COMING DOWN
THE ROAD
with Jesus

BILL TUCKER

ISBN 978-1-0980-4230-1 (paperback)
ISBN 978-1-0980-4231-8 (hardcover)
ISBN 978-1-0980-4232-5 (digital)

Christian Faith Publishing, Inc.
832 Park Avenue
Meadville, PA 16335
www.christianfaithpublishing.com

Cover Photo by Teri Tucker Poitedint

Printed in the United States of America

I want to start this book by giving thanks to God, for He has blessed me so much in my life. I was saved by His marvelous grace when I was about eighteen years old through the sharing of Jesus by my precious mother. She told me all about Jesus. She made sure we attended our church, Calvary Baptist Church, in Moultrie, Georgia. It is because my mother shared the Lord with me that I have Him in my life today, and I know He will keep me forever. I am so grateful to her for telling me about Jesus.

My mother, Ruby Marie Tucker, had been ill for a couple of years. The only thing the doctors told the family was that she had arteriosclerosis. In March 1961, at the age of 59, she died from a cerebral hemorrhage. This was devastating to me since I loved my mother very much.

I pray that God will help me to remember what is right and will keep me on the path of truth.

> "But they that wait upon the Lord shall renew their strength; they shall mount up with wings as eagles; they shall run and not be weary; and they shall walk, and not faint" (Isaiah 40:31 KJV).

Great-Granddaddy

GREAT-GRANDDADDY TUCKER

In 1066, William the Conqueror, Duke of Normandy, and his army crossed the English Channel and defeated the English at Hastings. He became the first King of England: William I. Some of the men in his army were crowned knights for their bravery.

One of these men was Henry Touderouer. Over a three-hundred-year period, his name, after several generations, was changed to Tuker and was finally changed to Tucker.

The first Tucker, Henry of Dartmouth, landed here in 1829.

Henry Crawford, Sr. moved to Tallahassee, Florida. He cut the first trees down to build a log cabin. He also set up the first legislative body near where the capitol of Tallahassee now stands. Henry Crawford Tucker Jr. is believed to be with his dad at that time.

Henry Crawford Sr. and Sally Hunter Tucker were Henry, Jr.'s parents. It is believed that Henry, Jr. and his dad were very close and that his dad helped him build his house in 1818.

He obtained some of his land through a grant, and he also purchased some of it. I have heard that he owned land from the Bay Community to Moultrie and that he gave each of his children so many acres of land.

Henry Crawford Tucker, Jr. was born in South Carolina in 1805. He traveled to Montgomery County by covered wagons. This reminds me so much of the series *"Wagon Train"* on television.

He was my parental great-grandfather. He was a tall, slender, well-built, blue-eyed man. When he said grace at the table, you could hear a pin drop. He was a well-known primitive Baptist minister, and he raised the largest family of the pioneers.

My great-grandfather was married three times: his first wife was Nancy Sapp, the second Margaret Watson, and the third Rebecca Bryant. He had a total of thirty-two children: eight by his first wife, eleven by his second wife, and thirteen by his third wife.

Sadly, two of the children died when they were young. One of the children, a nine-year-old girl, fell into a kettle of hot water as she played near the kettle. Henry was devastated and fell on his knees and prayed that God would forgive him for leaving the girl alone at the mill.

One day my greatgrandaddy went into Lazarus Department Store in Moultrie, Georgia. He told Mr. Lazarus he wanted to purchase thirty-two hats for his thirty-two children. Mr. Lazarus said, "if you have thirty-two children, bring them in and I will give each one a hat."

Well, granddaddy did take the children to the store. He lined all thirty-two of his children up in front of Lazarus Department Store. Sure to his word, Mr. Lazarus gave each one a hat.

My father, Wright William Tucker, was his grandson. His second wife, Margaret Watson Tucker, was my father's grandmother. My father's father and mother were James S. Tucker and Susan Murphy Tucker.

At the time Henry Jr. built his house, there were Indians in the territory. The Indians would come up near the house just to watch him work. They would follow him but would always keep a distance between them since they respected him.

Henry Crawford Tucker Jr. was ordained into the Gospel Ministry by the Sardis Church. He served in many churches in the area for many years. During his sermon one day, he preached on patriotism, and afterward, a man named Johnson came and talked with him. He told my great-granddaddy that he wanted to go fight for the South, but he didn't have anyone to take care of his family. My great-granddaddy told the man to go and serve and that he would take care of the man's family. He built a one-room log house beside his home to take care of Johnson's family while Johnson fought in the war.

My great-granddaddy also built cabins back of his house for his slaves, a grist mill, a commissary, a blacksmith shop, and a carriage house.

I understand that the Tucker home is a historic site, but in trying to visit it a few years ago, we found that some member of the family now has it, and we were unable to go onto the property.

His slaves were freed in 1863, but some of them chose to stay with him.

I understand that he formed several churches in the area: Bethel in the edge of Brooks County, Bridge Creek, and Sardis. He also had brothers who were preachers.

One year, his biggest crop was wool from his sheep. He dug two wells—one for his stock and one for his family.

When the War Between the States erupted, the forces of the United States of America and the Confederate States of America fought a long, hard, four-year war. Colquitt County was four years old when Fort Sumter was fired upon.

The census of 1860 showed only 204 families living in the county.

My great-granddaddy was also a captain in the militia. As their captain, he would send two men ahead of the troops, scouting for them as they moved out. He told the scouts to keep their eyes open and when they saw the Indians to get back as fast as they could. They moved on, knowing that at any time they could come upon the Indians and the battle would begin.

It was about 10:30 a.m. when they heard gunfire. About thirty minutes later, the scouts returned, telling the captain they had come upon the Indians at Warrior Creek and that it would be about a thirty-minute ride on horseback.

Captain Tucker spoke with authority. "You men, off your horses, out of your wagons, and form a scrimmage line north and south."

They did so, and started moving out through the bushes and trees. After about forty-five minutes to an hour, the sound of a rifle was heard through the trees. The battle of Warrior Creek had begun.

About 4:30 p.m., every man attached to the militia gathered at the Tucker home. Captain Tucker made sure every man had plenty of ammunition, a bedroll, and something to eat since he did not know how long they would be gone. One of the scouts found the Indian trail and followed it until it was too dark to travel. They knew the Indians wouldn't travel in the wilderness at night, so Captain Tucker told them to pull the wagons side by side to make camp for the night.

They made a hitching post between two trees for the horses and mules, and made sure they were secure for the night. They built a fire and ate. They sat around the camp-fire, not knowing if some of them would be killed the next day.

The next morning, Captain Tucker gathered the men around him. The men were silent and stood with their heads bowed while Captain Tucker prayed before going into battle.

Henry Crawford Tucker fought his last battle with Indians, between what is now known as Moultrie and Adel on the Warrior Creek in 1834. Indians were on their way to join another tribe in Florida. They had found some white women who had been scalped, so they attacked the Indians, thinking they were the ones who had done this awful thing.

Chaos fell on the land. Trouble was brewing in every direction, and it fell right on this man. The militia made him a captain, and he served so faithfully. He gave his all for God and his country, and he would fight for liberty.

The War Between the States lasted from 1861 to 1864. The Georgia Ordinance of Secession was signed in January 1861. Captain Tucker voted to secede from the Union.

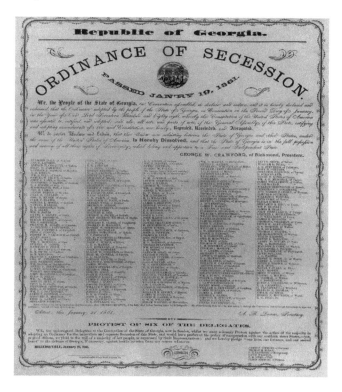

My great-granddaddy lived at his home near Moultrie until his death. He was killed when his horse became frightened and he was thrown to the ground. Great-granddaddy did not die instantly. He lived for a while until complications set in. He was 81 at the time of his death.

This is a sketch of Henry Crawford Tucker's house which was done by W. Ronald Tucker, great grandson, grandson of Jasper Davis Tucker (30th child) and Matte Sloan Tucker September 1990. This sketch was provided to us by Ms. Bridwell from Moultrie, GA.

ELDER HENRY CRAWFORD TUCKER'S HOME.
CIRCA LATE 1820'S-EARLY 1930's (MOULTRIE,GA)
SKETCH BY W. RONALD TUCKER (GREAT GRANDSON,
GRANDSON OF JASPER DAVIS TUCKER (30TH CHILD) AND
MATTIE SLOAN TUCKER, A SEPTEMBER 1990.

THE LEGEND OF CRAWFORD TUCKER

(Lyrics by Bill Tucker)

He was born in 1805, so the legend goes
Thirty-two children by three wives
Blessed by the Lord, don't you know.

His name was Crawford Tucker
A pioneer of the land
He had a dream, and he had a smile
And he was a preacher man.

A circuit-riding preacher
Who preached the Word of God
Throughout the night and through the cold
Just to win a lost soul.

Then came the War Between the States
Chaos fell on the land.
Trouble was brewing in every direction
And it fell right on this man.

The militia made him a captain
He served so faithfully
He gave his all for God and his country
And he'd fight for liberty.

Then came the day God called him away
His journey on this earth was finished,
But he left behind a legend so fine
And a dream that really came true.

My paternal grandfather was James Soloman Tucker, born in 1852 He was Henry Crawford Tucker, Jr.'s sixteenth child. He was married to Susan Murphy, and they had ten children. Five boys: Timothy, Robert, Tommy, Wright, and General. Five girls: Maggie, Callie, Mary, Ella, and Mattie. Wright Tucker was my father.

I think I was young when my grandmother and grandfather died, as I cannot remember anything about them.

My maternal grandfather and grandmother were Bo and Nancy Strickland. They lived until I was in my twenties. They lived in Coolidge, Georgia. I was only able to visit with them a few times, but it was hard because we did not always have reliable transportation, and we lived around forty miles from them.

My Granddaddy Strickland was a man of large stature and a devout Christian, and he raised his children to be respectable individuals. He died when I was stationed in California with the Marine Corps.

My grandmother was a large woman, and one day, when she was walking in the yard, she fell and said, "Jesus," and she died. She was a great Christian lady.

They had five children: Lester, Zaulton, Ladson, Ruby Marie, and Mamie. Ruby Marie was my sweet mother.

BO AND NANCY STRICKLAND

My dad, Wright Tucker, was a hard worker. He share-cropped with our help for several years. When he stopped sharecropping, he went to work at the Moultrie Cotton Mill. My mama was such a caring and loving person, and would fix Daddy's meals. I would carry the meals to him. Daddy worked on the big spinners that you put the thread on. After he had worked at the mill for several years breathing in all the dust and cotton, he developed emphysema and finally had to quit his job. After this, he went to live with my brother Wayne and his wife, Elaine, and he would visit around with the rest of his children for short periods.

My dad passed away on June 3, 1977 (my birthday). Wayne and I were talking with Dad just before he died, and I asked him if he had given his life to Jesus. He told us that he had. This made his death a lot easier as we knew we would see him again.

DADDY AND MAMA WRIGHT AND RUBY MARIE TUCKER

My mother was Ruby Marie Strickland Tucker (she was called Mae). She was one of the best mothers you could find in the world. That is exactly how sweet she was. She loved the Lord dearly. Most of the time, she would talk with us about Jesus and tell us to live a good Christian life. She worked in the cotton mill a couple of times. I don't recall how long she worked there, but she had to quit because of health reasons. My mama passed away in March 1961.

Mama and Daddy had eight sons and three daughters: Dolphus Mathew Tucker, Madison Junior Tucker, William James (Bill) Tucker, Wayne Donald Tucker, Dewey Ray Tucker, William Larry Tucker, Douglas Tucker and Daulton Terry Tucker; and Nadine Tucker Justice, Pauline Tucker Justice, and Nancy Winifred Tucker Hawley.

All but one of the sons enlisted in a branch of the military, except Douglas, who died when he was three years old. Wayne, Larry, and Daulton served in the Navy. Ray served in the Air Force. Junior and I served in the Marines and Dolphus served in the army.

Me, Myself, and I: Bill

I was born in 1930, about seven miles south of Moultrie on what was then called the Old Post Road. My Aunt Ella and Uncle Ave lived near us. All the roads were red with Georgia clay. We lived up this winding clay road about a half mile. Even then, that old house was very old. We lived there about a year or two. Then we moved to the cotton mill village. It went by that name at the time daddy went to work in the mill. The place we lived in has been torn down for many years. I can recall the house was old and shabby, with shutters for windows. You could see through the cracks in the floor. If my memory serves me right, it was about one-fourth mile off a dirt road.

When I think back to that time, I see lifestyles were so much different than they are today. It was hard times back then. I don't think we spent much time thinking about it. Mama and Daddy did the best they could to survive with what they had. At that time, they had six mouths to feed.

When I was a teenager, our family moved to my Uncle John's farm to sharecrop. Uncle John lived on a small hill. He was married to my Aunt Mary, who was my daddy's sister. We moved into a wood-framed house about one-fourth mile from Uncle John's house. You could barely see his house from ours because of all the trees and curves in the road.

Uncle John and Aunt Mary would sit on their front porch (both dipped snuff). When they would see someone coming down the road, they could not tell who it was until they got closer. This is how I came up with the title for my book. Every time Uncle John and Aunt Mary saw someone coming, one or the other, would make the statement that "someone was coming down the road."

About another half-mile down the road, my dad's brother, Uncle Tommy, and his wife, Aunt Jewel, lived. Then farther down the road was where my good friend Grady Sloan and his mother and dad lived.

Grady's daddy had an old truck. He was working on that truck all the time just to keep it running. When Grady and I started going places together, we didn't have a vehicle, so I would talk Grady into asking his daddy to borrow his truck. Most of the time, he would let Grady use it—that is, when it was running.

One Sunday, when we went to church, there were pretty twin girls singing a special. One of the girls caught my eye. Oh, I thought I was in love. After church, all of us just hung around and talked. I told the girls I liked their singing. I asked one of them if they would like to go out sometimes. She said she would talk to her sister. She came back and told me they would go out with us. Grady got his daddy's old truck, and we picked the girls up.

The only time we went out with the girls, they wanted to know where I lived. I tried to fool them, by having

Grady pull into a circular drive of some people I knew. The man who owned the house with his wife was a farmer. The house was very big, and it was made of brick. The girls' eyes got so big when they saw the house. The girl I was with said, "Is that where you live?" As with all jokes, they must come to an end. I told her no, this was not really my house. Then they wanted to know where I really lived. So we took them to a shotgun house that really looked bad. Grady pulled into the yard and immediately backed out. Between the shotgun house and the old half-running truck, this was our last date.

Grady and I joined with a group of other boys to form a baseball team. We would play against two or three other teams. I was one of the pitchers on our team, and Grady was the catcher. Four of the boys were called up to play in the county leagues, which would be equivalent to college baseball teams now. We had some excellent players on our team. Since our teams played on Sunday, my mother did not want me to play baseball because she did not want me to play on the Lord's Day.

Bill's Family Moved to Poulan and Bill Met Joan

My family moved to Poulan, Georgia, in 1949. One day, when I went to the school to pick up my brother Ray, I saw this girl who was in the class with Ray. I asked him if he knew her. He told me she was an "uptown girl" and wouldn't have anything to do with me. I saw her again one day when she was skipping down the street (if you know Joan, you would think she is skipping because when she walks, she walks so fast that it looks like she is skipping), in front of the Gray's house on the way home from school with her jeans rolled up.

On another day, I saw a group of girls at the old well that was downtown Poulan. Joan Seago was one of these girls. I asked her if I could go to her home to see her. Another girl was Vivian Ford, who was Joan's friend. I asked if Wayne could come too. They said yes, and we went to Joan's house. The first night Wayne and I visited with Joan and Vivian, I saw a piano and asked who played. Joan stated she did. She was asked to play something. She played "My Happiness," which became our favorite song, even to this day.

I was a little concerned about Joan's daddy not liking me. There were two front doors to her house. When we were in the living room, he would come into the bedroom door and kind of grunt when he went past the living room. He finally got to the point where he would speak to me, but it was more like a grunt than a salutation, so I figured he did not like me seeing his daughter.

At the beginning of our friendship, I didn't think Joan's mom liked me either. She told Joan I looked like a little boy.

I wanted to see Joan every day, but my daddy didn't know what to think about it. We only had one vehicle, and I had to wait for my turn to use it.

ENLISTED

I enlisted in the Marine Corps in 1951 in Macon, Georgia. I was sent to Paris Island, South Carolina, where I attended boot camp. That was hard times. We had sergeants who would drill and march us from sunup until sundown. Almost every place we went, we had to run.

In the beginning, our heads were shaved. They wanted all of us to know that we were changing civilian life to the military life since we were enlisting in the Marines.

Once we were out on the beach, they made us stand at attention. Some type of insect would fly around our faces and bite us. We would have to blow and twist our noses to keep them from biting. We could not move, as the sergeants were watching and would remind us to stay at attention and let the bugs bite. Believe me, that was horrible.

BILL TUCKER

Soon after enlisting, I met James "Andy" Anderson, and we became friends. He told me he did not have any family. It appeared other guys did not want him around. When our boot camp training was over and we were placed on leave, I invited him to go home with me, as I knew my parents would accept him since he was a friend of mine. I introduced Andy to my girlfriend, Joan, and her family. He was very comfortable around both families.

Andy was younger than me, but sometimes, when he wasn't around me, he would drink alcoholic beverages. I would talk with him about this, telling him he really shouldn't be drinking.

When we would be in line waiting on chow, he would push his way up the line to get to me, and he would get in trouble. I told him he shouldn't do that; he would upset people who had been waiting in line for a long time.

My maternal grandfather, Bo Strickland, died toward the end of the year, and I came home but did not get there in time for the funeral. I loved my grandfather and grandmother dearly, so I spent some time with my grandmother. Andy was home at the same time.

On Saturday night, he called my girlfriend, Joan, and asked her if I was already at her house. She told him that Junior and I were picking her and Vivian up and we were going to Albany. I had seen Andy awhile before leaving Moultrie, and he had a bottle of whiskey in his back pocket. I told him again that he shouldn't be drinking.

Junior and I picked Joan and her friend Vivian up in Poulan, and went to Albany. Joan and her mother spent the night with Joan's brother and sister-in-law, Buford and Lavon Seago, and Vivian and her mother spent the night with relatives in Albany. After our dates, we took both of our girlfriends to these locations and traveled back to Moultrie from Albany.

On Sunday morning, Leo Pritchard—sheriff of Worth County—called Joan's home, and her dad told him that Joan and her mother had spent the night with Joan's brother the night before. He gave Buford's phone number to the sheriff.

Leo Pritchard called and talked with Buford, who told him that Joan and her mother had spent the night with him. Leo asked Buford if Joan knew James Anderson, that he had been found beaten to death and her picture was in his wallet. She informed him that she did, and explained that he was visiting with my family. Joan called me, and Junior and I went to Sylvester to identify the body.

His body had been placed beside a road that was a shortcut into Poulan. If Junior and I had taken Joan and Vivian back to Poulan on Saturday night, we probably would have found his body.

The Provost marshal talked with Junior and me at length regarding where we were, what we did, what we wore, who we were with, and what kind of vehicle we were driving.

On Monday morning, the marshal visited Joan and Vivian at Sylvester High School, where they were both students, and asked them the same questions.

Several days after James's death, his body was being transported (not sure where to). There was a curve called Dead Man's Curve between Sylvester and Poulan, where the ambulance wrecked and threw James's body out of the ambulance onto the pavement. This all seemed like a nightmare.

I learned that James did have a grandmother, and Joan and I corresponded with her for several years.

Several years afterward, I was talking with someone who worked at the Marine base who told me that they were still working on this case but had not charged anyone with the murder. At this time, I do not know if the person or persons responsible for his death have been charged.

ANDY ANDERSON

STATION IN CALIFORNIA

In the latter part of 1951, I went out on leave with some friends, Loran Ticknor, and Keith Loran. Both were drinking. I always refused to drink with anyone, as I have always felt it was the wrong thing to do. That night, an ex-marine, Richard O. McAlister, approached us, telling the two who had been drinking that he had something in his apartment that was good for a hangover. He talked us into going to his apartment.

After we arrived at his apartment, he began fixing something for the ones with a hangover. I tried to talk with my two friends, telling them that they shouldn't take what he was preparing, but they did not listen, and both drank what he had prepared. I had a glass of milk, but I placed a napkin over it so no one could pour anything in it.

Soon after the two drank what he prepared, both were getting sick. I noticed they were both getting sicker and sicker, so I told them, "Let's get out of here and get a doctor." We left and went to a doctor. Keith Loran died while Loran Ticknor survived. Ticknor later told me that they should have listened to me and shouldn't have taken the supposedly "hangover cocktail."

During the trial of Richard McAlister, I was called as a witness against him since I was at the scene and was the only one who was not drinking.

This is an article from a newspaper in California. The actual article would have been shown here, but it is so old it is hard to read:

DELAY GRANTED IN MARINE POISON DEATH HEARING

A marine who swallowed poison last May 17 as a supposed "hangover cocktail" and who survived while his buddy died, yesterday reviewed his miraculous escape with the fatalism of the fighting man.

"That pill just didn't have my name on it." Said Pvt Loran J. Ticknor, 22, as he appeared as a witness for the arraignment of Richard O. McAlister, 22, of 1206 Miramar Street, on a charge of murdering Pvt Keith Loran, 22, of Seattle.

Pvt. Loran died last Monday in Corona Naval Hospital from the corrosive effects of swallowing a capsule containing 5.1 grains of poison, an autopsy showed. He leaves his widow and two children in Seattle.

Hearing postponed

Municipal Judge John G. Barnes postponed McAlister's preliminary hearing until next Thursday to permit the Public Defender to prepare its defense.

While I was stationed at Camp Pendleton, California, my brother Wayne was in the Navy at a naval base there. I had the opportunity to visit with him. I went into the base and tried to locate him. I was told which barracks he was in. I saw him coming down some steps from his barracks. I stepped aside so he would not see me. As he got to the bottom, I jumped up and grabbed him by the arm. I said, "Hey, boy, what are you doing?" He was surprised to see me.

We went out on liberty together; He and I were always wanting to do things.

"Hey," I said. "Let's exchange uniforms so we can see how I would look as a sailor and you would look as a Marine."

He was a little taller than me. When he put my Marine Corps uniform on, it was too short on him, and when I put his naval uniform on, it was too long on me. We just walked around a lot and had a good time just being together.

One night, a friend of mine and I were eating in a restaurant when we noticed an older couple not too far from us, and who was sitting at a table that looked as though it was not as comfortable as the one where we were sitting. I went over to their table to ask them if they would like to trade tables with us. They stated they were fine where they were seated and thanked us for thinking about them. When my friend and I went to pay our bill, we were told that the older couple had paid it for us. This was certainly a nice gesture for them to do this for us.

KOREA

We were scared and didn't know what to expect when we got off our ship, the *USS Marine Lynx*. We got aboard trucks to go inland. From Seoul, Korea, we drove about thirty-five or forty miles to a place called Kemp Peninsular, just a short piece from the river that separated North and South Korea. We could hear some big guns firing in the distance. That was enough to make goose bumps all over you, being the first time close to combat. As the days moved into weeks and months, we found the shelling and bombing wasn't all that scary since we had foxholes to get into and we knew where the enemy was.

Early one morning, about daylight, Hinson, Sergeant Bo, three other Marines, and I went out. The sergeant was the only one who knew where we were going. I carried a 30-30 machine gun, one Marine had a Browning automatic rifle, and the other Marine had rifles. It was a little scary at the beginning. After a few hours, we all settled into a quiet walk through the trees up the hills and heavy, tall grass. Everything was going fine. We reached the place. The sergeant got his information and said, "Let's go home, men."

Approximately halfway back, we were moving through a thick side of a hill, pine trees about head high, the grass almost that high. We were quiet. Suddenly, the sergeant who was moving out at the point came running back. "Hit the deck, be quiet," were his words.

He began to tell us there was a troop of North Koreans at the bottom of the hill we were on. We would have come out right where they were if we had not heard them. He said, "Don't even breathe hard. If they spot us, we have a fight on our hands." No one even whispered. We were too scared. We just looked at one another and got set for the worse.

It seemed as though they would never move out. I was glad it wasn't too cold or raining or snowing. It was bad enough just the way it was. Being caught in a position like this would put a bad taste in your mouth, or you would feel sweat popping out on your forehead, and I don't know how many things ran through my mind.

The sergeant went off to check after we had been there for about four hours. When he returned, he told us to move out, stay low, and be quiet. We were as quiet as deer the rest of the way.

It was cold that afternoon in February 1953. I was with the First Marines. My outfit was stationed out on the Kemp Peninsular and along the Kempo River. The main command post was on the Peninsular, the river that separated South Korea from North Korea. The first night we were there, we were greeted about four times that night with bombs all around us.

I had guard duty four hours each day. Occasionally, a lieutenant would come to check us out to see how alert we were. This particular night, I was guarding an ammo dump.

It was cold, so I got back off in a corner where no one could see me, and held my rifle up and pointed it toward the entrance to the ammo dump, which was barbwired in.

Suddenly, I heard a noise coming toward the dump. I saw only one man, and he was jumping from side to side on the path leading to the dump. All I could think of was a group of Koreans coming in on me, so I prepared myself for a fight. Those few minutes went by, I got to thinking I only had eight rounds in my rifle, and I placed a couple of clips filled with bullets where I could grab another one just in case.

At that time, this person had gotten to the front of the ammo dump. I was even scared to say, "Who goes there?" as I pointed my rifle toward him, and he didn't answer. I released a bullet, ready to fire.

The person said, "Easy, Tucker, it's me, Lieutenant [can't remember his name]."

I told him to come toward me so I could recognize him. He was looking down the barrel of my rifle when he got to me. He told me I did not have to worry about him checking me anymore.

One day, I was called up to Captain Willie's office. I stepped inside his tent and saluted him. I said, "Tucker reporting, sir." Captain Willie asked me if I knew how to drive. I said, "Yes, sir." He handed me a piece of paper and told me to take it down to where the jeeps were kept and to give it to the person in charge. He said, "Get in the jeep and turn it around." I did this, and he told me that I had my jeep. He already knew the jeep was for Captain Willie. He just wanted to know if I could drive. I got in the jeep and went back to Captain Willie. Captain Willie told me he wanted me to be his driver. Everywhere that Captain Willie went, I went.

Reconnaissance patrol was often in this place with this outfit. The sky was dark, and it was snowing. I knew if anything happened the rest of my squad would be here with me real soon. That made me feel a little better. I still had the gut feeling that anything could happen, like it had so many times before. I was in what we called an outpost on a high hill overlooking our command post. I could hardly make it out on this mountain looking down at the command post because it was so dark.

We had a foxhole deep enough and very wide so you could easily stay hidden and see all around you. In the daytime you could see for miles, but at night you had to keep your eyes open, just in case the North Koreans decided to come calling. I was camouflaged in a foxhole about four feet deep, and it was getting darker by the minute. That morning it was my watch. I was there from midnight until 4:00 a.m. God let everything be okay that night.

That night, everything went smoothly, except I was getting wet and cold. My replacement came, and I returned to the command post. I had made it back again without being fired upon.

DJ Hinson was my good friend and buddy. He was in special services. He had multiple jobs to do. Sometimes I would help him with sorting the mail for each company, then it had to be delivered to about three companies out along the Korean River, where they were dug in to keep the North Koreans from coming across that river. There was quicksand all up and down the river, making it impossible to cross.

We felt pretty good, knowing if they tried to cross it, it would be hard to do, and we could fight them off. They knew this, so they never tried to cross the river the whole time I was there. It didn't stop them from firing across the river with everything they had, and that was a lot. They would come over at night in small airplanes, drop their bombs, and return to their companies. They never found our command post, but they came close a few times.

DISCHARGED FROM THE MARINE CORPS AND ON TO MARRIAGE

On March 23, 1954, I completed my tour of duty and was discharged from the Marine Corps. I returned home to Moultrie, Georgia and could not wait to get to Poulan, Georgia, where my girlfriend, Joan Seago, was waiting for me. She was completing her high school education in June, and we planned to marry soon thereafter.

On June 2, 1954, Joan graduated from Sylvester High School. At her graduation, she was one of the top 10 graduates and received the typing award for her typing abilities.

On June 23, 1954, Joan and I were married. Early that morning, we went to the courthouse in Sylvester to purchase our marriage license. Since she was not twenty-one years of age, they refused to sell us a license.

We immediately went to the Ordinary's office in Thomasville. They sold us a marriage license since we told them Joan was eighteen years old; however, Joan was not eighteen until the following January. We did not have to have proof of our ages.

We returned to Poulan with marriage license in hand and went to the Methodist Parsonage, where Mrs. Taylor, the pastor's wife, had decorated the room where we were married. During the ceremony, when Reverend Taylor said, "You may place the ring on his hand," I held up my left hand, but Joan pushed it down and took my right hand. I guess she was so nervous she couldn't tell right from left. I still have the same ring. While working, I got my ring finger caught, and it scared me so much; therefore, I carry my ring on my car keys to this day. The ring still looks brand-new.

Article written by Mrs. Taylor, Pastor's wife.

Your ring was the symbol of the unbroken circle of love. Love freely given has no beginning and no end. Love freely given has no giver and no receiver. You are each the giver and each the receiver. Your ring always calls to mind the freedom and the power of this love.

Bill Tucker and Joan Seago were united in Marriage on July 23, 1954 at United Methodist Church parsonage in Poulan Ga. By Rev. Allan. Witnesses were Mr. & Mrs. Bill Branch and Mr. & Ms. Dolphus Tucker.

Joan still has the same rings I purchased for her before our wedding. She says she will never get rings to replace them. I did purchase her another diamond for her fiftieth birthday, and she wears it on the same finger with her wedding rings.

After the wedding, Joan and I went to the car and found two men sitting in the backseat. We soon realized it was two friends who were just playing around with us. We tossed them out.

We left the Methodist parsonage and met our wedding party at H. V. Thompson's place in Sylvester, Georgia, where we talked and laughed until around 10:30 p.m. We left there, traveled to Thomasville, and found the Piney Woods Cottages and rented one for a couple of days.

You and me forever!

OUR LIFE

Married July 23, 1954 at the parsonage of The Poland Methodist Church. The Worth County Probate Court would not allow us to get married since I was not 21 years old

We had a "Secret Love Song"

BILL AND JOAN'S WEDDING

PINEY WOODS COTTAGES, THOMASVILLE, GA.

PINEY WOODS COTTAGE

Restaurant in Poulan

In 1955, I opened a small restaurant/doughnut shop in Poulan, Georgia, where I started making doughnuts to see how well I would be able to make them. They had an excellent taste, and everyone who purchased them talked about how good they were. I served hamburgers, hot dogs, and French fries. The cotton mill was in operation at that time, and I would take orders at the mill and deliver the food for lunch and supper.

Recently, Joan saw Janice Carter, who lived in Poulan during that time. She told Joan that the doughnuts I made were the best ones she had ever tasted. This made Joan's day, and she couldn't wait to get home to tell me what Janice had said.

I have kept the original copy of my business license, even though it has been over sixty years.

BILL'S CAFE

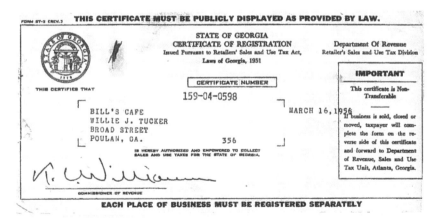

BUSINESS LICENSE

Hazel and Bill's Wedding

Joan's sister, Hazel Seago, and Albert (Bill) Branch were married in Omega, Georgia, in 1956. The same preacher that married us also married them. Brother Taylor had moved to Omega, so Joan, Donna, and I traveled to Omega to attend their wedding. It was a simple but nice wedding. Joan told me that if it had not been for Donna, who was then one year old, she would have cried all during the wedding. Having Donna with us and with her cute ways she was able to fight the tears back.

During this time, we lived in a two-bedroom, one-bathroom house in Poulan that was owned by Lacey Welch.

Joan's sister, Hazel, worked at the bus station in Sylvester. Bill and Hazel talked with us about moving in the house with us for a while until they could locate another place to live. We all agreed to that, and it worked out fine.

Hazel's husband returned home from work each day before anyone else. He would cook supper; often, he would make pots of soup. When he made soup, he would always want me to taste it when it was done to make sure it tasted good. He would use different types of beans, plenty of tomatoes, and I'm not sure what else he used, but it was always good.

Hazel and Bill lived with us around a year. When they found a place to rent, they moved out. We always got along good.

One time, Joan, Hazel, Teri, and I traveled to Nashville, Tennessee. That night, when we arrived, we went to a motel restaurant. We looked at the menu. At that time, the hamburgers at this restaurant were $2.85 each. I was not aware that hamburgers would cost so much since we could buy them at home for $1.25. I looked at everyone and said, "Let's get out of here, I'm not paying $2.85 for a hamburger." We left, and all of us were laughing so hard that I started driving down a one-way street the wrong way. When I saw cars coming toward me, I turn around right in the middle of a bridge and went back the other way. It's just a miracle the police did not see us and that we did not have a collision.

CHRISTMAS-BOB SEAGO SANTA

One year, when our children were little, Joan and I decided we would take the children somewhere, and asked someone to play Santa Claus and place their Christmas presents under the tree while we were gone. Our nephew, Bob Seago, agreed to do this for us. When we came home, our children walked into the living room and saw all the gifts under the tree. They were so excited because Santa had been there.

Construction Work

For several years, my brothers and I did construction work. Most of the time, we would have jobs within our living areas, but at different times, we would have to go to Florida and Auburn, Alabama, to work.

When we were working in Florida, both of my girls, Donna and Teri, were anxious to go with us since they really loved the beach. Also, Tony, my son, worked with us some during the summer when he was not in school. The girls would tell me that they would cook for us and help us if we would just let them go. Of course, both the girls cooked us good meals.

I remember one time when we were returning from Florida my brother Junior was driving his car. We had stopped and eaten lunch when Tony decided he wanted a milkshake. This was not a great idea as Tony always had problems with being lactose intolerant. After about two hours, he released gas, and Junior got a whiff of the scent floating in the car. Junior immediately pulled down into the ditch, jumped out of the car, and said, "What is the matter with you, boy? Don't you ever use the bathroom?" Finally, after a little while, the car was aired out, and we continued on our way home.

I had been having trouble with terrible pains at different times while I was at home but got to feeling better before we were supposed to go back to Florida to work. I traveled back on Sunday, but on Monday, I got deathly ill with pain again. Junior called Joan and told her that he would take me to Valdosta, and she should meet us there as I was really sick.

Joan traveled to Valdosta to pick me up. When she saw me, she said that she would take me directly to the hospital in Albany, as I was in such severe pain. By the time we reached Palmyra Park Hospital I was feeling better, so I told her to take me on home. She refused to do that, and I ended up being admitted to the hospital.

The doctors did a lot of tests, and after several days, they decided that I had a kidney stone and it was lodged between my bladder and kidney, and I would need to have surgery to remove it. I was in the hospital ten days during this bout. After the surgery, I was not able to return to work for about three weeks.

One night, several months after this kidney stone attack, I had another one. The pain was so severe at the time, so Joan and I kneeled in the hallway and prayed that God would take the pain away and heal me of these attacks. Praise be to God, He took the pain away and healed me. Until this day, I have not had another kidney stone attack, and I give Him the praise and glory for this healing.

Vacations

When our children and my brother's children were growing up, all of us would take vacations to Florida together. We would rent cottages on Lake Weir at Ocala, Florida. All the children looked forward to these vacations as they had a great time while visiting there. We would usually go during August when everyone could take a vacation.

I remember one time when we were traveling, we stopped at a roadside park and spread our lunch on the tables. Each family had cooked, and we had quite a feast. Joan had made a 1, 2, 3, 4-layer cake iced with Hershey cocoa, and it turned out to be a fantastic-looking cake. Just as soon as this cake was set on the table, a huge spider ran right across the middle of it. Joan was so upset about the spider, but Junior looked at her and told her that he was going to eat that cake, it didn't matter if a spider had run across it. We did eat the cake, and Junior said that was the best chocolate spider cake he had ever eaten.

After we arrived at our destination, all our children would go to the pavilion. This was a place where they could go, and you could feel that they were safe. It was not like it is today. If I had young children today, I would be afraid for them to be left at a place like that without our supervision.

One year, when we went to Lake Wiere, we rented a house from Carolyn Griffin, who worked with Joan. It was a real nice place, and we enjoyed it very much.

This was before my brother, Ray Tucker, died. Ray, Mike, Teri, Joan, and I went out on the boat one morning. We managed to get on a bed of fish. Every time all of us would throw our reels out, we would immediately catch fish. This happened all day long, and we were all very excited. Ray had thrown his line out and laid has reel down to bait another hook. When he laid it down, a fish bit and pulled the reel into the water. I started the boat, and we chased that fish down and caught him. We were all so excited about the way the fish were biting that day, but we have never had that experience again.

One year, before we went on vacation, we decided to purchase a new vehicle. We went to the dealership, picked out one that we wanted. Joan had made arrangements with the credit union in Atlanta to purchase the vehicle. We went on vacation, and when we returned home, the credit union had called and stated that they would not finance it because it had been a rental car. We took the car back to the dealer and told them what the credit union had told us. They took the car back since they knew they had not told us the truth about it.

COSMETOLOGY SCHOOL

In 1963, I attended cosmetology training at Albany Technical School. During that time, we moved to Albany until I completed my training.

While I was in training one day, one of the students went to the reception area and called for Mrs. Boody. There was no one there by that name, so she went back and looked at the appointment book and realized the thing that was written was *body wave*. Everyone was so tickled about what had happened we kept laughing all day.

After I graduated, I went to Atlanta and rented a duplex apartment and purchased a couch. A stove and refrigerator were furnished, and we moved our furniture from Albany to Atlanta. I went to work with Marvin and Marion McDaniel and my brother Wayne at a beauty shop on Virginia Avenue. My wife was working in Atlanta with the state Department of Education, mathematics division.

My mother-in-law, Mrs. Seago, was very unhappy about our move. I think she was unhappy about our grandchildren not being near her as she loved them dearly. Joan was upset about the way her mother felt. After Joan went to work in downtown Atlanta, she would come home every day telling me her neck hurt all the time. She finally stopped worrying about the way her mother felt about our move, and her neck pain subsided. She made the decision that since our immediate family was all together, that's what really mattered.

Carbon Monoxide Poison

When my family lived in Atlanta, one weekend, the weather was extremely cold. The temperature was three below zero, and it had snowed. We were not accustomed to weather like that as we had always lived in South Georgia, where the weather was mild. On this particular Saturday, we had been inside all day, and none of us felt good. That night when we started to bed, we decided to sleep on our hide-a-bed instead of in the bedroom. My brother Ray was at our house, and he went back to one of the bedrooms to sleep.

Joan and I placed our children between us on the hide-a-bed, but all three of them were restless and could not go to sleep. We thought maybe all of us might have the flu.

About three o'clock in the morning, Ray came from the bedroom to the kitchen and passed out. Joan stumbled back to one of the bedrooms and called my brother Wayne, who lived just a few miles from us. She told him that all of us were sick and might have the flu, but he said he would be right over to check on us.

When Wayne arrived and opened the front door, he said, "Let's get out of this house! There is a gas leak!"

We left the house and went to Wayne's house to stay until we could have the gas leak checked.

I will always believe it was a miracle of God that kept all of us awake. If we had gone to sleep, we might not have awakened. If Ray had not passed out, we probably would not have called Wayne. It is only by the grace of God that our family is alive today.

After I had almost two years of cosmetology experience in Atlanta, we decided to move back to the Albany area. I came back to this area and lived with Joan's mother and dad until June 1967, when Joan was able to get a transfer back to Vocational Rehabilitation Services in Albany.

A couple of months after we returned to Albany, I applied for a loan to purchase a car. I was turned down. I asked the lender why I was turned down. He told me that I did not tell him that my wife and I had been separated. They had found that I had been back in Albany and Joan had still been in Atlanta. I explained to them that we were not separated. Joan was waiting on a transfer back to Albany so I lived with her mother and daddy for about three months while she was waiting on the transfer. After that was settled, I was able to purchase the car.

After several months, I decided to open my own beauty shop. The shop was in a small building, but when the Midtown Mall was built, I rented space and purchased new equipment since it was a much-larger place. I hired several hairstylists and shampoo girls. I can still remember some of their names, but that was many years ago: Carol Walters, Amy Sullivan, Barbara Barwick Apon, Gail Kirksey Moree. These were all great to work with.

Sometime after opening, there was another shop being opened, and the operators were waiting for their place of employment to be finished, so they approached me about working in my shop until theirs was completed. They were with me for several months.

During this time, I was approached by someone from WALB-TV about styling the weather girl's hair for some free advertisement. The two ladies that I recall were Vicki Graves and Dora Griffin. They would come in every day before going on the air. I would style their hair, and at the end of the weather program, my shop—Styles by Bill—would be advertised.

Buying First Home

As soon as Joan's transfer could be made, we rented a house for over three years. We wanted to purchase a house in another area, so I started talking with some of my patrons who lived in that area. I asked them to let me know if they knew of any houses for sale. One day, Liza Wood came into the shop and asked me if my wife and I would be interested in looking at her house in that area. We made arrangements to go to see it that afternoon.

After looking the house over and talking with Liza and her husband, Hill Wood, regarding cost of the house, we decided to buy it.

The next morning, Joan called the State Department of Education Credit Union, where she was a member, and borrowed the money for the purchase. We thoroughly enjoy living in the area.

During the 1970s there were several deaths in our family: my dad, Wright Tucker died on June 3, 1977 (my birthday); Joan's mother, Lois Seago, died June 26, 1977; her dad, Ben Seago, died June 18, 1978 (Father's Day); and her brother, Buford Seago, died October 2, 1979 (Jerry and Donna's anniversary).

Property in Putney

My brother Wayne approached me about purchasing some land in Putney on Highway 19. We purchased a piece of property on the corner of Highway 19 and Broach Avenue. I do not recall the exact size of the property. We kept it for several years and sold it to Judson and Betty Hand, who built a house on it and lived there for several years before they decided to build in Fort Gaines on Lake George.

PURCHASING CHINA CABINET, TABLE AND BUFFET

One day, I was out working in the yards when I saw our next-door neighbor Stella Burke carrying some furniture out. I asked her what she was doing with it.

She said, "I don't want it anymore, I am going to burn it."

I told her I would give her $100 for the china cabinet, buffet, and table. She told me she would be glad to sell it to me. I purchased them. It was not a very pretty color at the time, but I stripped all three pieces and varnished them. When I finished them, they were three pretty pieces of furniture. She did not have the chairs with the table, so we purchased six chairs from Badcock Furniture.

My sister had purchased a new china cabinet, and when she saw ours, she told us that she would trade with us. We really didn't want to trade since we liked ours.

> "But unto every one of us is given grace according to the measure of the gift of Christ" (Ephesians 4:7, KJV).

Property in
Mitchell County

We ventured out several times and purchased property. We learned about fifteen acres in Mitchell County that was for sale. We looked the property over. It seemed like a great deal, as there was quite a bit of timber on the property. We contacted the bank and purchased the property.

We would go out and reminisce about what we could do with the property. We thought about building a house on it, but it was a little too far from any town. We did not want to be that far from everything.

Periodically, I would go to the property alone. One day, while I was walking around checking things out, I heard a gunshot. I looked around and saw a man with a gun. I yelled at him and asked what he was doing. He did not answer but fired another shot. He was far enough away from me that I could not see him clearly to know who he was. I left as soon as I could get to my vehicle. I never found out who he was, but nothing like that ever happened again.

We had some good neighbors there, the Darbys, who had a son named Tim who was good friends with our son, Tony. Mr. Darby owned an airplane, and he and Tim would get Tony to go flying with them. I remember the first time Tony flew with them. They did not bring him home as early as we thought, so we were quite worried. All we could think about was that they might have had trouble with the airplane, or maybe it might have crashed. Around 9:30 p.m. they called, and we were relieved to know that they were all right.

Mr. Darby went to the store one night and was killed in a car crash on Gravel Hill Road. Since that time, Mrs. Darby and Tim returned to their home in another state. We have not heard from them since, but I hope if they ever see a copy of this book they will try to get in touch with us.

We were approached by our neighbor J. T. Gordon, who asked if we were interested in selling this property. His dad wanted to purchase it. We told him we would be glad to sell it to his dad. Arrangements were made, and Mr. Gordon purchased the property and built a real nice home on it and lived there for many years.

FOUNDATION

In 1977, we were members of First Baptist Church of Putney. A group of teenagers were interested in forming a gospel group, and they approached me about being their manager. They were all around seventeen and eighteen years old. The group consisted of Bobby Apon, Frank Massey, Daryl Salter, Beverly Stanfield (singers), and Johnny Farr (pianist). The vocalists and the pianist were very good. I agreed to manage this group. We booked them at different churches around the areas of Albany, Dawson, Columbus, and Camilla, and they were well received.

A short time after we started the group, they approached me about cutting a record. Wayne and I had a Cross Country Label, so we decided this was a good idea. We cut a 45-vinyl record with one song Bobby had written ("Me and the Master") and one song Wayne and I wrote ("It's My Fault").

That was quite an enjoyable time, as all these young people were Christians and their families were excited about their endeavor and supported them 100 percent.

FOUNDATION

Twenty-Fifth Wedding Anniversary

On our twenty-fifth wedding anniversary, Donna and Jerry asked us to go to their home in Moultrie and eat supper that night. Joan, Teri, and I went, not knowing that they had planned something for our anniversary. After supper, Donna brought out a wedding cake and told us happy anniversary. This was the first wedding cake we had since we did not have a large wedding. This was a complete surprise, and we appreciate their thoughtfulness very much.

25TH WEDDING ANNIVERSARY

BRENDA REDD

When we were members of the First Baptist Church of Putney, our preacher and his wife, J. B. and Joyce Redd, had a daughter, Brenda Redd, who was a very attractive young lady who had a gorgeous voice. She was also a great pianist and was majoring in Voice at Albany Junior College at the time. Since I have written a lot of country music songs and have been trying to find someone to record some of them, I asked Brenda's parents if they had any objection to Brenda singing country music. They had no objections, so my brother Wayne and I talked with her about cutting a record. She was very excited, and so were we.

We immediately started making plans to have Brenda sign a contract with us to cut a record. We already had a copyright on the ones we wanted her to record, so it was just a matter of going to Nashville and getting connections with the best recording studio there.

Brenda was always at ease when she was singing. She is just a complete natural because she enjoys it so much.

Brenda, Joan, Wayne, and I went to Nashville to cut the record, "You're All I Need" and "For Old Time's Sake." We spent two days in the recording studio with some of the best musicians accompanying Brenda on that record.

During the time we were there, one afternoon, we were watching the news, and it was a very sad time as President Reagan was shot that afternoon. We could not believe that something like this would happen. We were all pretty much devastated.

On the second day, we had to leave as soon as the recording session was over in order to get Brenda back to Albany the next morning, as she had a test. We traveled all night, and she was able to take her test that morning. I know she was tired, because the rest of us were.

After this record was cut, Wayne and I contacted a promoter in Nashville to promote it. The best I can remember, his name was Charlie Lamb. He promoted it for several weeks, and "You're All I Need" went to number 13 on the charts.

Brenda and Joan were guests on *The Ralph Emery Show* in Nashville one morning, and they visited radio stations to promote the record. They were having a ball doing these things.

We were members of the Country Music Association. I was never one to talk very much, so it was always easy to get Brenda and Joan to participate in different things, such as doing promotions, etc. We bought tickets to the *Country Music Association Awards Show*, and Brenda and Joan attended. After the show, they attended the party where all the country music celebrities were and got to meet several of the big country music stars.

The following is an article found in one of the newspapers soon after "You Are All I Need" was released:

Cross Country Records is proud to introduce a new country music artist. This is a young lady we think has a good chance of becoming country music's next sensation. We would like to introduce you to 21-year-old Brenda Redd of Putney, Georgia, who is currently attending Georgia State University, majoring in music. She has been singing since an early age and is working hard at her singing career. Her voice is similar to the style used by Debbie Boone, Anne Murray and Emmylou Harris but she copies no one. Her voice is smooth and easy to listen to and professional all the way.

Brenda attended Furman University in Greenville, South Carolina, for one year. On her last day at Furman, before returning home for the summer, she got into a jeep accident on the Furman University campus. Her worse injury was to her mouth. Doctors were concerned that her speech would be affected to the point that she might not be able to pursue her singing career, but due to her love for music and her determination and enthusiasm, she was singing again three or four weeks after the accident.

Brenda has performed in Little Albany Theater productions. She has sung with the state band in high school, with the jazz band at Albany Junior College, and at college functions at Albany Junior College and Furman University, and she has appeared on local television on special occasions.

Brenda's new release is "You're All I Need" written by Bill Tucker (Putney, Georgia) and Wayne Tucker (Pelham). The flip side is "For Old Time's Sake," written by Larry Tucker (Atlanta, Georgia) and Billy Ray (Perry, Florida).

BRENDA REDD

BILL AND WAYNE TUCKER

RECORDS

HARDENS

In 1985, I began playing rhythm guitar with the Harden Brothers in a Blue Grass Gospel group, which was a fine group of men and one woman. We performed at the nursing home every Tuesday night and would go to different churches when asked.

One night, Rod Craven was emceeing. He was announcing the song they would be singing. Before I knew it, he said, "Bill will sing the first verse, and I will sing the second one."

I had never sung in front of a group, so I almost croaked when I heard him say that. We started playing, and I started singing. I was so nervous, but everything turned out fine. If I had had time to think about it, I would have really messed it up, but thanks to God, He was right there with me and everything was okay.

THE HARDENS

DIXIE PROPHETS

When I left the Hardens, I joined a group of gospel singers known as the Dixie Prophets. This group was made up of Tommy Marchman, James Ireland, Lavern Bennett, Randolph Pate, Eunice Weems, and me. I played rhythm guitar with this group. This group sang at numerous churches in the area.

We all wore the same kind of suits (even loud colors—pink and red). We were a sight! Our wives would travel with us to most of the sings and they enjoyed being at the sings as much as we did.

After the sing, we would load the equipment. By this time, we were all getting hungry. We would head over to Shoney's in Tifton. I am a homebody, so Joan and I did not go all the time. We did go once in a while. It is funny, Joan is a goer and I am a stayer. Her switch is set to go 24/7.

We saw many souls saved at the sings. That is what it is all about. We love Jesus and wanted others to have the same love we have.

THE DIXIE PROPHETS

Seago-Tucker Family Restaurant

In 1987, Joan and Lavon Seago, Joan's sister-in-law, were traveling from Sylvester to Albany when they noticed a building for rent on the Sylvester-Albany Highway. Since Lavon and her deceased husband had been in the restaurant business for years before his death, they thought it would be a good idea if we looked into renting that building to open a restaurant. Joan came home that day and talked with me about it.

We started securing information about how much it would cost each of us to go into that business. We realized it would be very expensive since the deposit on the lights would be $1,800. I almost had a fit when I heard that, and said, "One thousand eight hundred dollars, are they crazy?"

However, we decided to go ahead with that endeavor. We opened the restaurant in the name of Seago's Restaurant, since Lavon and Joan's brother had been very successful in their past restaurants.

We had two of the best cooks we could have possibly had. Their names were Sammy and Myrtice. They had worked with Seago's Restaurant for many years. We were near enough to the Marine base and employees from the base would come to the restaurant to eat or to get carryouts.

One day, a long-haul truck driver was dining with us, and he told me that this restaurant and one in California were the best ones he had enjoyed eating at. He told me the food was always delicious.

In approximately two or three months, Lavon had an accident, which caused her to have some health problems, and was not able to continue to work. At the time she left, the name of the restaurant was changed to Tucker's Family Restaurant.

Soon afterward, our daughter and son-in-law, Donna and Jerry Willis, and their children, Mandy and Chris Willis, came to live with us. Jerry had been the minister of music and youth in a church in Columbus, Georgia.

During that time, Jerry was able to work with me at the restaurant. If it had not been for his being there, it would have been almost impossible to operate the restaurant. Joan was still employed by the state of Georgia and was not able to assist in the operation of the restaurant, except after her workdays and on weekends.

One of the men whom Joan worked with asked if Donna might be interested in going to work. He stated his wife worked with a Baptist Church and they needed to hire another secretary. Joan told Donna about the job, and she applied and was hired. Donna would go to the restaurant for lunch and after work and help with the meals.

At times, we would have the whole family working with us when they were not on their regular jobs.

In the beginning, we served lunch and dinner buffets for $4.25. We did not charge for tea or coffee. We soon realized that we would need to start charging 50¢ for drinks, and would you believe, the customers stopped drinking tea and coffee and started drinking water. I wonder how they feel about paying $2.29 for tea now.

I remember one day this man wanted tea, and I told him we had to start charging for it. He got upset. If I had really thought about it, I would have given him the tea. He was so upset about it. I don't know if he was on dope or alcohol. I thought we were going to have trouble with him, so I asked him to leave. He walked up and down in front of the building, but finally left.

On Friday nights, we would serve all-you-could-eat fish with the trimmings. We had gospel singers on Friday nights to sing and witness to the customers at the same time.

Joan's Fiftieth Birthday

On the day Joan turned fifty years old, I decided to have a surprise birthday party for her. Our children helped with the preparation. Since we had the restaurant at that time, it was easy to surprise her. We asked everyone to come about thirty minutes early so we could get positioned around the restaurant, so when she walked in, we all jumped up from behind the counter and sang "Happy Birthday" to her.

That afternoon, Donna and Joan went home. After everyone came in, Jerry, Donna's husband, called Donna and told her he could not find the keys to close the restaurant, that they would have to bring a set of keys back. Donna and Joan brought the keys back, everyone was in place behind the counters, all the lights except one were out, all the cars were hidden. When Joan and Donna walked in, the lights were turned on and everyone jumped up and sang to her. She was shocked as she had no idea what was going on.

Weeks before the surprise, the children decided that I should give Joan a new diamond ring. So all tips given were placed in a jar. The only problem was that the ring cost more than what they had saved. We ended up using the money as a down payment on the ring. Joan loved the ring, but because she was working, she ended up paying for the rest of the ring. Hey, it's the thought that counts.

We had such a good time at the restaurant as a family, but expenses were so great we finally had to close.

House Next Door

About eighteen years after we purchased our first house, our next-door neighbor Stella Burke decided to sell her house. We made arrangements to purchase it, but when it was time for us to close, she decided she did not want to sell.

Washington Trip

In 1992, our son-in-law Jerry Willis, who taught history at Byne, asked Joan and me to go on a senior trip with them to Washington DC. Since neither of us had ever been there, this was a great opportunity. We traveled from Byne Memorial Baptist Church to Washington DC by Southern Coaches. We left around 7:00 a.m. and traveled all day, reaching Washington DC after dark. We were very tired when we arrived, but the trip had been enjoyable as everyone was so congenial.

Jerry always had all the details worked out before leaving town. We had almost every moment of each day filled. I roomed with Jerry, and Joan, Donna, and Sylvia Broadaway roomed down the hall from us. One night, we heard a loud commotion down the hall, and Jerry thought it was some of his students, but lo and behold, when we learned who it was, it happened to be our wives and Sylvia who were making all the noise. The Braves had just won the playoff, and they were so excited they could not hold their emotions.

Not too long ago, one of the students on the trip with us, Jennifer Holliday Kraft, told Joan that when her mother found out we were going on the trip with them that she knew she would be all right, but Jennifer told Joan that the adults were the ones who got them in trouble.

We visited the US Capitol, the Smithsonian, the Lincoln Memorial, the Kennedy Memorial, the Changing of the Guards, Arlington National Cemetery, the Pentagon, saw the raising of the flag on Iowa Jima, visited the Ford Theater where President Lincoln was assassinated, the Vietnam Wall, and attended a dinner theater, where we saw a live production of *Annie*. This was a great presentation, and everyone in attendance seemed to really enjoy it.

We visited George Washington's home at Mt. Vernon. This was the highlight of the trip for me as it was quite interesting since I love history. The scenery was magnificent on the Potomac River. There were several houses, don't recall exactly how many, but every house we visited was breathtaking to me because I remember studying about George Washington. One thing that really amazed me was that George Washington had teeth made from wood. At the time I am writing this book, I have lost all my teeth, so I know how he must have felt.

There were small pots of shrubbery that you could purchase, as they were selling these pots to help with the maintenance on the property. I purchased one, and it still lives where I planted it when we returned.

The kitchen was placed in a building separate from the mansion, as there was a high incident of fire as they cooked on an open hearth. After the food was cooked, it was carried by the servants into the house.

The Washingtons had a riding chair, a chariot (a small coach and a light coach).

There was a smokehouse where hogs were slaughtered for food. The meat had to be smoked, dried, salted, or pickled because there was no refrigeration during 1776. The meat that was prepared there was eaten by the Washingtons or given to friends. They also had a problem with thieves, even though they kept the building locked.

The beds in all the houses seemed to be rather small during that period.

A large hemlock tree stands in the yard, which was planted by George Washington in 1785. The grounds are gorgeous with lots of huge trees and shrubbery, and the grounds are well-kept.

There was a washhouse where the family's clothes and guests' clothes were washed. They were dried behind the washhouse and ironed before being returned to the mansion. The clothes were labeled so there would not be a mix-up when the clothes were returned to the mansion.

There was a stable where they housed ten to twenty-five horses that belonged to the Washingtons, and guests' horses were also housed there. There were always hundreds of guests during 1785, thereby increasing the workload of the slaves and causing a strain on the Washingtons.

Purchase of Second Home

Fast-forward a few more years, Stella decided again that she would sell her house. In the meantime, she and her son, Dean Burke, had added a great room, another bedroom, and another bathroom. This made the house even more attractive to us. At that time, we decided again to attempt to purchase her house. We made an application for a loan. I never knew how much red tape there was to purchase a house. We finally told the people in the mortgage company that they knew more about us than we did. The loan was approved. Our daughter and son-in-law, Donna and Jerry, lived in the house for a little more than three years, but decided to move to another location.

Joan and I discussed moving to that house and renting our other house. We decided to do that since the newer location was larger. It had two bathrooms instead of one and had more closet space. We moved to that house in 1996.

Since we moved to the house next door, we have not had any problems in renting the other house.

A friend of ours, Eunice, told us that her son and daughter-in-law, Steven and Jennifer Martin, were looking for a place to move. We told her that the house is ready if they are interested. They contacted us and rented the house. Jennifer is a nurse at Phoebe Putney Memorial Hospital.

They did not live there very long as their son, Jonathan, was approaching school age, and they wanted to send him to Lee County School.

As soon as the house was ready to rent, Joan was in Debbie Baxter's office one day when Debbie asked her if she knew of anyone who had a house in Putney for rent. Joan told her that we did. She and her husband wanted to come out to see the place. An appointment was made for them, and they rented the house.

Debbie's husband, Randy Baxter, died after they had lived there for several years. He was visiting some of his relatives at the time of his death. Debbie lived in the house for thirteen years until her death.

After Debbie's family moved all her furniture out, Joan and I were cleaning the house, getting it ready to rent. Joan was in the Dollar General Store, and as usual, she always finds someone to talk to. She commented to this lady that she was purchasing cleaning supplies, that we had to clean a rental house and get it ready to rent. The lady asked where the house was located. Joan told her, and she said her son's family was looking for a place to rent and she would tell them. Joan introduced herself to the lady, who was Debbie Clark, and her son and daughter-in-law are Mike and Melissa Wilkerson.

Later in the day, Debbie, her son, and her daughter-in-law came by to see the house. They told us that they wanted to rent it. This is a great family who has become like family to Joan and me. They have three children: Tyler, Lakyn, and Briley. They have been living next door for over six years. Two of their children have become adults, and the other one is thirteen years old. They have always been well-behaved. It has been a joy for us to have these people as our neighbors.

Melissa home-schooled all the children. Tyler and Lakyn have already graduated from high school, and both have jobs. Tyler works with UPS, and Lakyn works with Phillips Clothing.

Mercedes Church Family Charles and Rita

Joan and I moved our church letter to Mercedes Baptist Church back in 1986. We have met some very good friends and have been very happy with our move to this church.

Sometime in the nineties, Rita Moulton asked Joan if we would be willing to help her and Charles, her husband, to clean the church every few weeks. We did not have a custodian to clean the church at that time, and each member was taking turns doing so. Joan told her that she would talk with me about it and let her know.

Joan asked me if I would be willing to help clean the church, that a friend at church had asked if we would be willing to help her and her husband. Of course, I agreed, and she told Rita we would be glad to help.

After we started cleaning the church, Joan would get home before Rita, so we would ask Rita and Charles to come to our house for supper. Joan would have it ready when they got home from work, and we could get to the church pretty early and it would not be very late when we finished cleaning. We did this for a long time.

After we hired a custodian, we did not clean the church any longer. We still got together on occasions for meals, and we all enjoyed being with each other. Since that time, they have moved to West, Georgia. We stay in contact with them. When we have homecoming at church, they always spend the Saturday night before with us. Rita always brings food for the homecoming, and she and Joan cook for homecoming on the Saturday night before.

They also visit with us at our lake home. We enjoy playing cards and just being with each other.

We were all in Church one Sunday when Ralph Gay came up to me. He said, "Bill, I just saw a headstone at Bay Cemetery of a Tucker man who had thirty-two children and three wives." Ralph asked me, while laughing, if that was some of my relatives. I looked at Ralph and told him that was my greatgrandaddy. Ralph had not heard the story before. We all had a good laugh then I told Ralph my story.

THE JOY SUNDAY
SCHOOL CLASS

The Joy Sunday School Class has the proper name. I know because I visited this "all women's" class. The ladies in the class include Dee Potter, teacher; Reba Benton; Ruth Gay; Kristie Johnson; Nancy Lamb; Myra Matthews; Bernice Mathis; Kay Royal (Class Secretary/Treasurer); Millie Spencer (Outreach); Joan Tucker; Donna Willis (substitute teacher), Joleen Price and Debra Brown.

Donna has to travel to Emory several times a year, Joan had gone with Donna and Jerry before he went home to be with the Lord. Joan continued going with Donna until she got to the point that she did not want to leave me alone at night (after all, I am 89 years young).

Beverly Davis stepped in and started going with Donna to Atlanta. After a couple of trips Beverly became very ill and could not make the trip.

Dee immediately offered to go with Donna and has been making the trips ever since. When Donna gets home she tell us about how much fun they had. Dee is good for

Donna in that she helps Donna look outward and not at her illness.

I wanted to put a story (and there are many stories and memories) about each church member but time ran short. Therefore, I want to tell each one of them I love and appreciate them. We have the sweetest fellowship.

THE DAVIS SUNDAY SCHOOL CLASS

I can't let Joan and Donna have all the fun. So, I am a member of the Jack Davis Sunday School class. It is made up of men and women. They include Virginia Rowe, Bobby and Colleen Chappell, Tom and Margaret (Margaret actually comes from the line of Henry Crawford Tucker) Mercer, Linda Collins, Martha Hannington, Freida Hewitt, Ronnie and Shirley Aubun, Frank Butler, Roger Royal, Roger Johnson. These people, like in Dee's Class are special, as is our whole church.

Purchasing Property on Pataula Creek

During the 1990s, Joan and I started talking about purchasing a place on the lake. We started looking at property on Lake Blackshear, but soon realized the property on that lake was quite expensive.

We contacted Liz and David Bullington, who had some property next door to some other friends, Ralph and Ruth Gay. They took us to see the land. It wasn't what we were looking for since it was not near the water. They also took us to see a house that Marcus and Delores Mulkey owned on the lake, but it was more expensive than we wanted.

We than started looking at Fort Gaines, Georgia, on Lake George. We contacted a realtor at Fort Gaines who showed us two or three places. It seemed as though the realtor did not think we were interested in buying property, and did not bother to call us again.

In 1997, we contacted realtors Babs and Rick Turner in Albany. They had a contract on a two-and-a-half-acre tract of land in Pataula Hideaway, which bordered the water. We traveled to Fort Gaines, which is about seventy-five miles away, to see the property. Water lines, a sewer system, and electricity had already been placed on the property. When they told us the price of the property, we decided to purchase it. We immediately contacted the bank and talked with Rosa Ramsey, with whom we had already done business with. We completed a loan application, and we were all set to purchase this piece of property.

During the closing of the loan, we were told that we might have to fence the property. Joan looked at me and said, "I don't think we need to purchase this property if there is a possibility that we may have to fence it, as that will cost a great deal to fence that much land."

The lawyer spoke up, "I think this is a great deal, and there may be a possibility you may never have to fence it."

We decided at that time to go ahead with the purchase. We purchased the property in November 1997. Shortly afterward, we purchased a three-bedroom, two-bathroom mobile home from a dealer in Moultrie, Georgia. The mobile home was eighty-six feet long, and the property was on a hill, which was on a corner lot where the deliverer would have to place the mobile home.

The first company who was contracted to deliver it could not get the mobile home on the property. All attempts were futile. Since they were unable to place the mobile home, they took it down to Tommy's Restaurant on Highway 39 and parked it for about three weeks.

Another company was contracted to deliver the mobile home. A representative of that company assured the trailer dealer that he could set the mobile home up on our property. He was successful.

Soon afterward, we started getting things done, such as connecting the electricity and water.

I contacted a person to build a dock and immediately started building a deck on the back of the mobile home. The mobile home was on a steep hill, so the deck was 14 × 32 and ten feet high. When I finished with the deck, it really turned out to be beautiful.

Nine years passed, and we enjoyed our time at the lake, but taxes were very expensive, so we decided to sell. Another reason we decided to sell is the fact that when we visited the property, all we had time to do was work. We never had any time for pleasure.

We contacted a realtor in Albany who knew a realtor in Fort Gaines. She stated he was very good at selling property on the lake. She brought the necessary contract for mine and Joan's signature, we signed it, and she mailed it to that realtor.

In less than a month, Joan answered the telephone, and it was the realtor calling. He told her that he had a buyer for our property. Joan told him she would have to talk with me to see if I still wanted to sell. I was mowing grass when Joan approached me and told me about the call. I thought for a few minutes, and since he told Joan we would be receiving the price we wanted for the land, if she was also willing that we would sell. We sold that piece of property on September 6, 2006.

GOPHER RIDGE RECREATIONAL PARK

My brother Junior Tucker and his wife, Margie, owned a mobile home at Gopher Ridge Recreation Park. This was closer to Fort Gaines where a lot of people had getaways near each other. We had visited them at that location and knew some other people who had mobile homes there. Junior had sold his, but we decided to look for a smaller place where we would not have to work all the time while were there. The yards at Pataula Hideaway were so big it took a lot of our time just cleaning yards.

We visited Gopher Ridge Recreation Park and started looking for sale signs. We noticed one on Lot 24. There was a sign that gave another address in the park. We contacted the lady who lived there. She informed us that Wayne and Jan Tiner owned the mobile home and she would contact them for us.

The Tiners met us a few days later to show us the mobile home. We decided that day that we would purchase it. There would not be much upkeep to the yards since they were very small. We had to provide information to the park manager, have a background check and a credit check before we could purchase the mobile home. This is a requirement of the park before anyone can purchase a getaway in the park. Everything was fine, so we purchased the mobile home. We took possession of it on October 1, 2006. At the writing of this book, we still own it and visit there as much as time permits.

A couple of years ago, the owners added $25 per month to everyone's rent in order to hire someone to mow all the yards. We have just received a notice from the owners that the rent will be raised to $200 per month beginning January 1, 2019. At this time, we are seeking another buyer.

We have made several friends at the recreation park since we purchased the mobile home there. We became very close to our next-door neighbors, Frank and Pat Hughes. Mr. Frank was gracious enough to come lend a helping hand to us when we would visit our place. He would help take our groceries and belongings into the mobile home. While I was adding another bedroom and bathroom on to the mobile home, he would lend a helping hand as long as he was able to. He had rotator cuff surgery and was out of commission for quite some time, but he was always willing to assist in any way that he could.

His wife, Mrs. Pat, became a real good friend to Joan. Joan would visit with her every time we were there. Joan learned that she loved salmon patties, but Mr. Frank did not like them, so almost every time we would go there, Joan would cook salmon and give Ms. Pat some. She was always appreciative, as she never cooked salmon.

Did I mention that Frank is the pastor of a church near the trailer? Joan and I would visit when we were at the lake. When the regular piano player was absent, Pat always asked Joan to play.

During the years Joan worked with rehabilitation service, she worked with one person who owned a mobile home there, Terry Hout and her husband, Bill. They had purchased a place before we did. We are sorry to say a couple of years ago Bill passed away unexpectedly.

PIANO RECITAL

Several years ago, Roger and Kay Royal were moving to Valdosta. Kay was the pianist at Mercedes Baptist Church, and this was leaving the church without a pianist. Someone in the church knew that Joan played by ear but had never had any formal training. They informed the pastor, and since there was no one else to play, they asked Joan if she would be willing to fill the position. This was hard for her and for the minister of music, Chuck Farmer. He was accustomed to having someone who had been formally trained. Joan was informed by Bobbie Anglin that she would be glad to teach her. Joan started piano lessons.

During one piano recital, Bobbie asked Joan and me to sing one of the songs I had written. We were both scared to death to try to do that, but we did. We secured a cassette tape of our song, and Joan said, "Oh, that was terrible. I will never attempt that again."

Joan gives Chuck Farmer credit for helping her through those years with the music. She states he taught her a lot during that time.

Fiftieth Wedding Anniversary

On our fiftieth wedding anniversary, our children secured the Georgia Power Building to have a fiftieth celebration. They made all the arrangements, prepared all the food, and invited a lot of our friends. It was a great celebration.

Our son Tony gave a little speech, where he told that Donna was born on the tenth of July and we were married on the twenty-third of July. He didn't tell that we had married a year earlier. Everyone laughed, as they knew he was kidding.

Another thing that I remember about that celebration was that they bought each of us an Orange Crush drink and pack of peanut butter crackers, since that was what we had during our honeymoon.

BILL AND JOAN'S 50TH WEDDING ANNIVERSARY

Joan's Retirement and Back to Work

Joan retired from rehabilitation services on June 30, 1991. She signed her first contract with the state and began work on August 1, 1991. She contracted for nine years, then decided it was time for her to completely retire. She was retired for one year when the pastor of the Mercedes Church, Russell Anglin, called a personnel committee meeting since the church secretary had resigned. Joan was on the personnel committee. They were informed that Shelby Doyle was resigning. Russell looked over at Joan and said, "There is one person in this room that could take this job if she would."

Joan looked at him and said, "I am not looking for a job."

They talked on for a while, and before Joan left, Russell said, "Think about it."

Joan told him she would go home and talk it over with me, and would let him know by Wednesday.

We discussed it and thought she would only be there for a short time. That short time ran into thirteen years.

Several years after Joan became secretary, I was approached about becoming a deacon. The pastor and other deacons talked with me at length. They stated that since Joan was secretary at the church it would have to be brought before the church to get approval for me to be ordained as a deacon since the bylaws stated that a deacon's wife could not be the secretary.

A meeting was called to bring this to the church. The church approved, and I was ordained as a deacon on February 23, 2003.

Lady—Man's Best Friend

In 2001, Mary Strawder and Myrtle Corley talked with Joan about a puppy they had found on the road that had been beaten. They took the dog to the veterinarian, and she was okay. Joan told them we did not want a dog. However, Joan decided to go to their home to see the puppy. When she saw her, she decided to bring her home. We both thought she was such a pretty and sweet puppy that we would adopt her. We named her Lady. When Lady was old enough, Joan took her to Obedient School.

Lady was always such a good dog. She never barked until she wanted to go outside. She always went to the side door and stood when she needed to go outside.

I took her out a couple of times and showed her the *Albany Herald* and asked her to pick it up and bring it to me. She started bringing the paper in every morning and would not give it to me until I gave her a treat. She was easily trained.

I would take Lady outside and teach her certain hand signals. When I would motion for her to go left, she would go left, and when I would motion for her to go right, she would go right.

Lady had a residual from where she had been beaten up when she was a very small puppy. She had hip dysplasia. When she was around fifteen years old, we talked with our veterinarian about some type of treatment for her. He did laser treatment on her several times that seemed to help some. However, in several months, she grew worse.

One Thursday afternoon, she had gone outside. We started calling her, but she did not come like she usually did. Joan walked about the house and found Lady lying on the ground. She could not move, and since she weighed about fifty pounds, we could not pick her up.

When our next-door neighbor, Mike Wilkerson, came home from work, I asked him if he would bring her into the house. He did, and laid her on the dining room floor. She could not move, and when Joan would sit down with her and rub her, she did not whine, but when Joan would stop rubbing her, she would start whining again. We knew she had to be in a lot of pain.

On Friday morning, she was not any better. We knew we had to do something for her, but neither of us wanted to have to have her put to sleep. We didn't do anything that day, but on Saturday morning, we made the decision that we could not watch her suffer anymore, so it was decided to take her and let the veterinarian put her to sleep. This was the hardest decision we have ever had to make.

When we returned with our sweet Lady, Mike, Teri and John Miller, Kayla's husband, came out to our home and dug a grave on the back side of our property for her burial. John and Teri had built her a box for her burial. She was with us for sixteen years. She was the best and sweetest dog we had ever owned.

LADY

My Eightieth Birthday

Joan knows I really do not like surprises. On my eightieth birthday, Mike and Teri invited us to have lunch with them. When we approached their home, I noticed a lot of cars. I looked at Joan and asked her what was going on. She did not say anything, just kept quiet.

When we left the car and started up the walk, a number of people started telling me happy birthday. I knew then my family had pulled a good one on me as I knew nothing whatsoever about anything.

There were family members, people from our church, and other friends. I wish I could remember everyone who was there, but there were so many I could not begin to remember.

WMU

Joan had invited the Women on Mission group to our home for a meeting. There were about eight or nine of the ladies in attendance. Everyone brought a covered dish, and they ate supper after the meeting. That night, when the meeting was ending, Joan was going to the kitchen to turn the coffee on when she stumbled and fell as she was coming up the steps from the living room. I did not know what was happening, but I heard someone say, "Joan just fell." I walked into the dining room, and Joan was on the floor and could not get up. This really scared me. Someone called the EMTs.

While we were waiting for the EMTs, one of the ladies, Ruth Gay, sat on the floor with Joan's head in her lap. She tried to make Joan as comfortable as possible. Ruth is one of the most compassionate people I know.

When the EMTs arrived, they took Joan to the emergency room. An x-ray was made of her shoulder, and she was informed that it was broken. They placed her arm in a sling and made an appointment for her to see Dr. McGee the next morning.

Joan saw Dr. Scott McGee the next morning. Another x-ray was made of her shoulder, and Dr. McGee informed her that she had a clean break and it had been decided that this type of break was better left without doing anything to it. She was told to be careful with it, and she did not need the sling. That was great news for all of us. Joan's shoulder healed, and she does not have any problems with it.

STRANGER INCIDENT

One Wednesday night after prayer meeting, when we arrived home, our next-door neighbor Melissa Wilkerson met us in the driveway. She stated a stranger came to our driveway a couple of times. He told her he was looking for someone on a street she had never heard of. He was told that he was on the wrong street and probably the wrong part of Albany.

He left but came back a couple of times. Melissa called the police and reported this incident.

When we had been home a few minutes, the man reappeared. I went to our back door and tried to talk with the man. It was apparent that he was either drinking or on some type of drugs.

The police were called again. The police came and sat on our dead-end road until midnight.

We should all thank our police for the service they provide, as we can always depend on them to do the right thing. Some people are not thankful for them, but it may be because these people are not trying to do the right things. Our police officers are underpaid for the job they do. They put their life on the line every day for the people they serve. Praise God each day of your life for our policemen.

Hurricane Michael

The first of October, we were warned that a hurricane was headed our way and it might be devastating. We immediately purchased food that could be prepared without cooking in the event we lost electricity, and saved enough water to last for several days. On October 10, a category 3 hurricane came through our area, causing much damage. This was a very long night. The lights went out before dark, the rain was pounding on our roof, and the wind was blowing very hard. Since we had no electricity and the air conditioner was off, it was extremely hot, we were perspiring. We began to talk about the day we were at the lake when a wall of wind came through. We thought that was a scary time, but this was much worse than that day.

We did not know the damage the hurricane had done until the next morning. A tree had fallen on our house over our bedroom. At our rental house, a tree had split, and part of the tree was hanging over the house, and part went into the pecan tree.

Josh Poitevint, our grandson, came from Perry the next morning to help clean up our yards. When he came into our house, he looked down and asked Joan what happened to her hand. It was swollen. We explained that we had removed the swing from the porch before the hurricane went through. After the hurricane, we hung it in the ceiling but did not notice the two chains on one side were not attached properly. After we hung it on the ceiling, Joan decided she would check to see if it was level. When she did, she fell on the cement porch. It was a miracle she did not fall off the porch as she fell right on the edge.

Josh called his mother, who was on a mission trip in Honduras, to tell her to call his grandmother and tell her to go to the doctor. We don't know what he thought Teri could do since she was so far away.

The accident had happened on Friday afternoon, and we figured it would be useless to try to see a doctor, and she would wait until Monday and see Dr. McGee.

Joan went to the doctor's office on Monday morning. They did x-rays and told her she had a cracked bone in her hand, and placed the lower part of her arm and hand in a cast.

One week later, the cast started hurting Joan. She scheduled an appointment to see why it was hurting. Two more x-rays were made, and a new cast was put on. Everything was better.

After our lights were restored, we had problems with our plumbing and could not get our tank to produce water. We realized our septic tank needed to be drained. After this was done, we still had problems, so a plumber was called. After checking everything, the plumber stated there was a lot of grease in the septic tank. He cleaned this, and these problems were resolved.

Power Outage

We had invited Mike, Teri, John, Kayla, and Tucker to eat with us. Joan started cooking in the morning. She had cooked peas, potato salad, and macaroni cheese. She planned to complete the meal during the afternoon and have it ready to eat when our guests arrived. About 3:30 p.m., our power went off.

Joan called Georgia Power to find out why the power had gone off since there was no bad weather and everything seemed to be okay. When she talked with the lady at Georgia Power, she stated there was an outage in our area and they would probably have it repaired by 6:45 p.m. Joan looked at me and said, "Oh no, what am I going to do? Our family will be here around five thirty."

Joan and I were sitting in the living room in the dark when Teri arrived around 5:00 p.m. She came in, and we told her what had happened. She sat in the dark with us until we heard John, Kayla, and Tucker coming in the back door.

As we approached the kitchen, the lights came on. They were able to finish cooking, and we did have our meal before too late. Since so much of it had been cooked that morning, it didn't take long to complete the meal.

My Brothers
and Sisters

Dolphus Mathew Tucker

My oldest brother was Dolphus Mathew Tucker. He was born in 1922. I recall one day he was drinking and got into a fight with a man, and he didn't realize the man's brother was with him. Both jumped on him and beat him so badly, that it took a long time for it to heal. Our family had to do our own doctoring at that time.

Dolphus settled down after that and was a sharecropper. After about two years of sharecropping, he enlisted in the army. He was sent to Germany. I don't know what company he was with, but he was involved in action and was wounded in his right foot. After he was wounded, it was a long time before he could walk. He finally received his discharge and returned home.

When Dolphus returned home, he met Ruth Swint, and they were married. He was employed by Swift & Company. After several years, he and Ruth divorced.

Around 1956, Dolphus met Hazel Waters, and they were married. They had two sons—David Mathew "Bo"

Tucker and Danny Ray Tucker—and two daughters: Brenda Tucker and Teresa Tucker Harvey.

They moved to Gainesville, Florida, where he retired and did a lot of fishing. He lived a good Christian life until his death in 1996.

DOLPHUS TUCKER

Nadine Tucker Justice

My oldest sister, Nadine Tucker Justice, was born in 1922. She helped our mother with some of our younger siblings. She married Tom Justice. They lived in Valdosta, Georgia, for many years. They had seven children: Thomas L. Justice, Otis Justice, Ralph Justice, Jack Justice, Robert Justice, Wanda Justice Pollard, Johnny Justice, and Martha Justice Harden. Martha passed away during the writing of the book. Robert was killed in an auto accident when he was a teenager.

Nadine was a special Christian lady who loved baking cakes and peanut brittle and helping others. Each time we would visit her, she would make sure she had peanut brittle to send home with us.

She had a wonderful life and is now with our Lord Jesus Christ.

Before Nadine's death, she asked me to write some things about our family so everyone would always remember us. So that is why I am writing this book.

NADINE TUCKER JUSTICE

Pauline Tucker Justice

My next sister was Pauline Tucker. She was born in 1924. She loved to sing, and she would get Nadine to sing with her while they washed dishes and cleaned the house. Nadine's husband, Tom, had a brother, Mack Justice, who started dating Pauline. It wasn't long before they married. They had seven children: Earnest Justice, Elsie Justice McMurray, Evelyn Justice, Ann Justice, Maxine Justice, Brenda Justice Crowe, Sue Justice Turner, Pat Justice, and Phillip Justice. Pauline was involved in church and sang in the choir. Pauline lost her husband after many years of marriage. She was devastated.

Just before Pauline went to be with the Lord, she told someone who was standing by her bedside that there was a man standing at the foot of her bed, another one at the door, and another one outside. We believe they were angels who came to take her to heaven.

PAULINE TUCKER JUSTICE

Madison Junior Tucker

My next brother was Madison Junior Tucker, who was born in 1926. He was a special kind of brother. Junior was away serving his country in the Marine Corps. When he came home after completing his boot camp training, I remember we were in the field stacking peanuts. We didn't know he was coming home at that time. I looked up, and Junior was coming across the peanut field. It shocked me when he looked up at me and threw me on the ground and said, "Hey, brother." I remember looking up from the ground and looking into his eyes.

After he returned to camp, he was hit in the arm by shrapnel.

PURPLE HEART

While in the Marine Corps, he married Laverne Griffin. During their marriage, they were blessed with four beautiful daughters: Debra Tucker, Barbara Tucker, Sandra Tucker, and Bonnie Tucker. Unfortunately, in 1958, they were divorced.

When Junior and I were talking one day, he told me about his experience as a Marine. He said one day they were out on a reconnaissance patrol. His squad of men were looking for the enemy. As they slowly moved through a rice paddy, a North Korean soldier jumped up out of the rice paddy just ahead of them.

Junior said, "He was about to shoot me, so I fired my rifle at him and shot him."

In talking with Junior, I could see in his eyes the pain he felt about what had happened that day. He was trained to do his job, and he did it well.

I don't know where he went after he was wounded, but do know he served his country well and was honorably discharged with a Purple Heart.

Junior married Marjorie Burgess in 1961. They were blessed with three girls and one boy. When the twins were born, they were unaware they were having twins when Marjorie went to the hospital. After the girl was born, the doctor went out of the delivery room, and the nurse called him back and told him there was another baby coming. He came back in and delivered the boy. This was a real surprise, as they did not know they were having twins, and this was the only boy. The children in this union are Jan Tucker Pollock, Meg Tucker Latham, Marty Tucker Greene, and Marcus Tucker.

I remember Junior always hosted our Tucker family reunion at his home for years. Some family members with several children would come in around 2:00 a.m., and he and Margie would have to get up and make room for everyone to sleep.

Junior would also buy meats and grill them for the reunion. After several years of doing this, he said, "That is enough," and he stopped hosting the reunion.

Junior always liked to go to a restaurant in Pelham to have breakfast with a lot of his friends. He was always friendly to everyone and always seemed to enjoy himself.

Junior was in an accident on the Old Pelham-Camilla Highway, not too far from his home. It was a sad day for all of us. Junior had to be placed in the Pelham Parkway Nursing Home after the accident. He was placed in the same room with his wife, who had been there for several years. Junior passed away on May 13, 2014.

Some time ago, I asked Meg to talk with her brother and sisters and get information about their dad that I might not have known.

Joan and I were in Meg's Shear Wonders recently and started to talk with Meg about her dad. She told us that Junior would come to the salon almost every day to see her, then he would go to Farmer's Bank to see Marty, then to Stone's to see Jan. He would always bring some type of fast food and would eat while he was at Meg's place.

Meg also told us that when her dad would see her on Saturday, he wanted to know if she was going to church on Sunday and if her business was fruitful. He was always so proud of all his children.

She also told us that her dad wanted to buy a new lawn mower every year. The last time he talked with Marty about it, she told him that he did not need another lawn mower, so he refrained from buying it at that time.

MADISON JUNIOR TUCKER

Nancy Tucker Hawley

Nancy was born in 1928 and passed away on November 2, 2015.

Nancy married Charles Hawley, who was in the US Air Force.

During 1958 and 1959, Chuck was sent overseas, and Nancy was not able to go with him. She lived with Joan and me during that time. She was pregnant with Doug. Since Joan's birthday is on January 5 and Nancy was due the end of December, Joan kept telling her that Doug was going to be born on her birthday. Nancy kept telling her that she hoped he didn't wait that long, but when January 5 rolled around, he was born!

My mother was sick during the latter part of 1959 and earlier part of 1960. Nancy lived in Moultrie and helped take care of her until she had orders to go to Morocco, where Chuck was stationed.

Since Nancy was a military wife, she was gone for nine years before returning to Georgia again. She lived in several places: Africa, Montana, Florida, California, Hawaii, and Pelham, Georgia. Nancy and Chuck had Seven children: Ginny Hawley, Doug Hawley, Janice Hawley, Tina Hawley Humphries, William Hawley, Melinda Hawley Worth, and Karen Hawley Haire.

NANCY TUCKER HAWLEY

Wayne Donald Tucker

Our family was beginning to grow even bigger. The next child was another boy named Wayne Donald Tucker, born in 1933.

Wayne enlisted in the Navy in 1952. He was not old enough to enlist, so our mama signed for him. He stayed in San Diego for about a year. Then, they put him on a tanker, the USS *Mispillion*. He was boatswain's mate. They would take care of the ships on the upper deck.

Wayne was on the five-inch gun, and he did high-wire rigging on the tanker. This is where they connected the hoses to high steel poles and the poles were lowered down the side of the ship to refuel. This was a big deal. No one was allowed on deck while fueling was being done. He was also on the lifeboat crew and on the captain's launch. They carried oil and supplies, and a lot of times, they carried beer. The beer had to be hidden and guarded to keep sailors from stealing it.

Wayne went all over the Pacific. There were a lot of islands where they dropped hydrogen bombs. After the bombings, their ship docked. The sailors were instructed not to eat the coconuts. But what did they do? They ate the coconuts!

He went to Hong Kong, Japan, and Taiwan. During all this time, they had an Indian on the tanker with them. The Indian's family owned land and ended up finding oil on that land. Boy, he was rich!

Wayne was coming off liberty one night, and he had had a few beers. He was headed to what he thought was his ship. He did not know that another ship, the *USS Tucker*, had docked in the harbor. Well, he went right on up to the deck of the *USS Tucker*. He ended up spending the night there.

The next morning, when Wayne woke up, he saw his ship headed out to sea. He stayed on shore all day long. When his ship docked, he told the officer in charge what had happened. The officer told Wayne that he had done the same thing himself.

I went to see Wayne when he was docked in California. The sailors were coming off the tanker, and I saw Wayne coming down the steps. He walked right by me. I grabbed him by the arm, and it scared him, until he saw it was me. He was really surprised to see me. We went back on board to eat. The sailors who cooked fed Wayne and me, and they gave us so much food. It was funny to see a Marine sitting in the mess hall with a bunch of sailors. They all treated me nice. They even played the the Marines' hymn.

Wayne went all over the ocean, even to Guam Island, where they dropped big bombs. Wayne said it was good to see all the places he saw, being a country boy, while in the Navy.

Wayne was enlisted in the Navy from 1952 until 1956.

When he was discharged, he came to live with us for a short time. During that time, he met Elaine Hutchinson, and they were married in 1959. They have three children: Andy Tucker, Julie Mills, and Serena Arnold.

During the time Wayne was in service, he met two other sailors (twins), and they became close friends. After their tour of duty, they went to cosmetology school and owned a beauty shop in the Atlanta area. After talking with them at length about the business, Wayne decided to go to school to become a hairstylist.

After he finished school, they moved to Atlanta, where he joined his two friends in the beauty shop.

During the time they lived in the Atlanta area, Joan, our children, and I would visit with them. We had a great time since Wayne and I were recording songs. I remember one night we were downtown and purchased a tape recorder. We were all having such fun with it until we really lost track of time.

After his family had lived in Atlanta for several years, they decided to return to South Georgia and settled in the Camilla-Pelham area. He opened a beauty shop in Camilla and was very successful with this endeavor. Many years later, he decided to sell his shop.

Serena Arnold, his daughter, and her two children came home to live with him and Elaine. After several years, she became employed in the Albany area, so she purchased a house in Lee County, and Wayne and Elaine moved with her since he had already retired.

In 2018, Elaine got very sick and had to be taken to the emergency room. She had to have emergency surgery. She has had a very rough time, but as I write this book, she is doing much better.

WAYNE TUCKER

Dewey Ray Tucker

After Wayne, another boy was born. He was named Dewey Ray Tucker, born in 1936.

He joined the Air Force when he was eighteen years of age. I remember one time he called to tell me he was stationed at an Air Force base not too far from where I was stationed at Camp Pendleton, California. We talked on the telephone, but we were never able to get together while we were both stationed in California.

After he was discharged, he had a child named Susan.

Sometime after that, Ray met Helen, and they were married. They had one boy and one girl, Thomas and Cathy. They were divorced when these children were very young. We have lost contact with these children and their mother.

Early one morning in 1985, I received a call from my brother Junior telling me that our brother Ray had been killed accidently. Ray was staying with a friend, and they got into a fight. The friend hit Ray on the head, and he died instantly. Since he had a brain aneurysm, he probably did not know what hit him. This was an accident, as his friend did not mean to kill him. This was one of the most terrible things that has ever happened to me.

RAY TUCKER

Larry William Tucker

Another boy was born in 1938. His name was Larry William Tucker.

When Larry was old enough to join the military, he enlisted in the Navy. I do not know anything about his military record but am very pleased that he did honor his country enough to serve.

Larry was married to Sandy Tucker, and they had one child, Stephen Tucker. They divorced when Stephen was very young.

Larry married Barbara, but this marriage lasted only a few years, and they were divorced. Larry had no place to go after this divorce, so I asked him to come to live at our place.

During this time, I did a lot of woodworking, such as building cabinets and refinishing furniture. Our congregation at Mercedes Baptist Church had sold our church building and had built a new one. Larry helped me build two modesty panels for our church choir.

He lived here for several years until he became so sick we could not handle him, and he had to go to a nursing home. He was in the nursing home for quite some time before his death in March 2013. During the time he was there, he always told me not to ever forget him. I told him that we would always remember him, there was no way we would forget him.

He was laid to rest at the Union Grove Baptist Church Cemetery.

Several weeks after Larry's death, we received a certificate honoring the memory of Larry in recognition of devoted and selfless consecration to the service of our country in the Armed Forces of the United States.

LARRY TUCKER

Douglas Tucker

The next baby was a boy named Douglas Tucker. He was born in 1940. Douglas developed diphtheria. At that time, not much was known about the disease. It really hurt us to see him suffer the way he did. I can still see his little face. He was such a sweet boy.

Before he developed this awful disease, each brother and sister took care of him. Our friends and neighbors were all very helpful to us by helping as much as they could. After all this, Douglas was called home to be with Jesus. Douglas died in 1943.

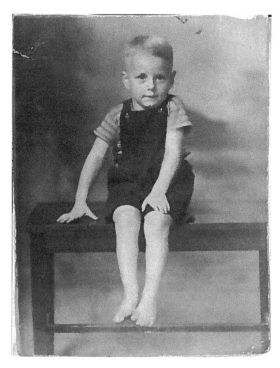

DOUGLAS TUCKER

Daulton Terry Tucker

After Douglas's death, another boy was born into the Tucker family. He was named Daulton Terry Tucker, born September 1946. He was another gift from God as he helped to fill the void of losing little Douglas.

When Daulton was eighteen years old, he joined the Navy on February 12, 1964. He was stationed in San Diego for twelve weeks of training. He said that all went well.

While Daulton was home on leave, he married the girl of his dreams, Carolyn Pollock, on May 11, 1964.

Then he got his orders for Adak, Alaska, which is located on Adak Island, where he was stationed for twelve months. Daulton heard that one of the motors on the plane he would be traveling home in had caught fire, and he got to thinking that could happen again. He said, "Boy, was I worried. I finally made it home. Only a military man could understand."

When he got his orders, he was assigned to the *USS Columbus*, which was the largest ship he had ever seen. It was a guided missile ship 950 feet long and 100 feet wide. He was really impressed. While aboard the *USS Columbus*, he was promoted to E4 and oversaw twenty men.

Daulton was on the Columbus CG-12 for two years which was a flagship that had a two-star admiral aboard.

His next orders took him aboard the new DD818, which was a destroyer. They proceeded to Vietnam, and it took two weeks to get to Subic Bay. They stopped to rearm there, where they loaded five thousand rounds of 5 × 38. Even though everyone on board helped, it took all day, and everyone was extremely tired. When they left Subic Bay, they left with a full load and arrived in Vietnam. They were on the firing line for three months.

Afterward, they were refueling helicopters. Daulton told me that was a sight to see, a forty-foot helicopter right beside the ship. He told me he never thought about how dangerous it was.

Daulton was discharged from the Navy on January 16, 1968. He later learned that he had made E-5 if he would ship over for six years. He thought about doing that, but the decision was made to not reenlist.

Daulton and Carolyn have three children: Daulton Todd "Sonny" Tucker, Lori Tucker Justice, and Scott Tucker.

DAULTON TUCKER

Our Physicians

Dr. Melinda Greenfield, Dermatologist

I have a dermatologist that I have been seeing for several years. She is Dr. Melinda Greenfield. She is so thorough when detecting skin cancers. The first time I saw her, I had a tiny speck on the side of my nose. She immediately did a biopsy. When the results of the biopsy came back, she called me in to schedule surgery.

Surgery was scheduled as soon as possible for Mohs surgery. A surgeon Dr. Rooney, from Atlanta, actually performed the surgery.

My daughter, Teri, went to see Dr. Greenfield for her yearly body scan. Dr. Greenfield performed the scan and noticed a tiny pin-tip spot. She told Teri she needed to biopsy the spot. As soon as the report came back, Dr. Greenfield had to tell Teri that the small spot was a melanoma. Of course that scared us all.

Teri had to go back and they did another biopsy and removed a larger section of her upper arm. We praise the Lord because the biopsy came back clear. Now, more of my family gets body scans.

Dr. Latifat Agbeja and Nurses

Joan and I had lost our primary care physician that we had been seeing. She retired so we had to find another doctor. Our daughter suggested her doctor, Dr. Latifat Agbeja. We made our appointments and began seeing Dr. Agbeja.

My daughter had an appointment with Dr. Agbeja. While Joan was at the office with Donna, she decided she would take the flu shot (never had one before). She came home telling me all about it. She said she did not even feel the shot when Makayla, the nurse gave it to her.

A few days later I looked at Joan and said, "I thought you would go with me to get the flu shot." She looked at me and said, "I did not know you were planning to take it."

After we talked for a while, I decided that I would take it. You have to know that this was a big step for me because I have never had one in 89 years. We saw the same nurse, Makayla. She is such a nice nurse and she knows how to give a shot that does not hurt. The physician and her group of girls are the best.

Our Children

Donna

In 1955, we had our first child. Joan was in labor for about twenty-four hours. During that time, Joan's mother, Mrs. Seago, and her friend Mrs. Ford were at the hospital waiting for our baby to be born.

A nurse came out of a room and motioned for me to come to that room. I immediately went to see if she had some news for us about our baby.

She said, "You can come in to see your wife."

I walked into the room, picked up supposedly my wife's hand. Immediately, I realized this was not my wife. The lady was around thirty-five years old; my wife was only eighteen years old.

I looked at the nurse and said, "This is not my wife."

She said, "You don't know your own wife?"

"Don't you think I would know my wife."

She said, "If this is not your wife, get out of here."

I left the room and saw Mrs. Seago and Mrs. Ford down the hall laughing as they realized what had happened when I left the room.

Our oldest child, Donna Jean Tucker, was born at 7:45 p.m. She was a beautiful blue-eyed blond girl.

When Donna was three years old, we moved from Poulan, Georgia, to Moultrie, Georgia. Shortly after moving, one night, Joan had fed Donna, given her a bath, and laid her on the couch. Within a few minutes, Joan looked at Donna and noticed she was scratching on the couch. She told me to watch what Donna was doing.

I took one look at Donna, picked her up, and told Joan we needed to take her to the hospital. We lived about three or four miles from Vereen Memorial Hospital. That was the longest three or four miles I have ever traveled. Joan and I were both traumatized as we did not know what was happening to our child.

The doctor ran tests and stated Donna had a convulsion. She was admitted to the hospital. The next morning, when she tried to walk, she would stagger. The doctor really did not know what caused her problem. He wanted to know about her activities that day. We knew she drank a Coke from a can. He thought she might have gotten something from that but did not know.

About three months after that incident, the same thing happened again. After she was released from the hospital, we decided to get an appointment with a pediatrician, Dr. Findley, in Albany. Donna was examined by Dr. Findley. He secured an appointment with the Georgia EEG clinic in Macon, Georgia to have an EEG to get a proper diagnosis.

Donna was taken to the Georgia EEG clinic, where they diagnosed her as having grand mal epilepsy.

During our next visit to Dr. Findley, he informed us about the diagnosis, and he said she would probably outgrow this condition if we would do exactly as he instructed us. We kept regular appointments with Dr. Findley and followed all his instructions. Donna was placed on phenobarbital and Dilantin for several years. At the age of twelve, she was dismissed and has never had any more seizures.

When Donna reached eighteen, we purchased a yellow Pinto car for her. One day, she decided to wash her car, so she connected the hose to the water faucet in our front yard. After she finished, she did not disconnect the hose. She decided to go to a friend's house and did not notice the hose was still connected to the faucet. She drove off and pulled all the plumbing from under the house. Boy, that was a mess, and Tony and I had to replace all the plumbing.

She had gotten very rebellious and wanted everything her way. She left home on her first day of the twelfth grade, and we did not know where she was for several weeks.

Joan and I did some soul searching, and realized we were not being faithful to God as we had stopped going to church and were not raising our children to worship the Lord, as we should have. We were both Christians but had not been faithful. The fact that Donna had left home really brought us back to the Lord, where we should have already been.

We started going to church, and we will always feel that the Lord let this happen to get us back on the right track.

One day, Donna called her mother and wanted to return home. Her mother told her that she could come home if she wanted to follow the rules and regulations of our home, but otherwise, no.

She came home. That week, we were having revival at First Baptist Church of Putney with the Rev. Dick Sharp preaching.

The first afternoon Donna was home, she, Joan, and Teri had to pick me up in Pelham. While on the way to Pelham, Teri looked at her mom and said, "I want to accept Jesus as my savior."

Donna said, "I don't want something like that."

However, that night, we attended the revival. When the invitation was given, Teri went to the left and Donna went to the right from our pew. They both met down at the altar and both accepted Jesus as their Lord and Savior. That was a very happy time for their mother and me.

Jerry Willis was our minister of music and youth. He and Donna started dating and were married six months later in 1976 at the First Baptist Church of Putney. After their marriage they moved to Griffin, Georgia, where he had accepted a call to the Southside Baptist Church.

In 1977, a beautiful baby girl was born into their family. Her name is Amanda Michelle Willis. Joan said she was one of the most beautiful babies she had ever seen. They waited at the hospital for her to arrive until the wee hours of the morning.

When Mandy was six weeks old, we were visiting Donna and Jerry who lived in Tifton. When we were getting ready to leave, Joan looked at Mandy and said, "We need to take you home with us."

Jerry looked at Donna and said, "Get Mandy's clothes ready."

Joan was thrilled when he said that, as she thought Jerry would not want us to take her to Albany with us. It was a Labor Day weekend, so Donna and Jerry came to Albany on Monday to get Mandy.

We were so thankful that they were willing for us to keep Mandy. Since Jerry was music and youth minister, when they would go on trips with the youth, we would be able to keep Mandy while they were gone.

In 1983, Jerry and Donna where serving at a church in Columbus, Georgia. They were so happy at the church. The choir was full, and the youth department was large.

Donna got a job working as a paraprofessional at one of the local schools. She worked with kindergarten and first-grade students. She worked with Connie Marriott. She really enjoyed that job and working with Connie.

One day, Donna became sick and stayed that way for several days. She finally made an appointment with the doctor. You might have guessed: she was going to have another baby.

Things were going along so well for Jerry and Donna. They loved the ministry they were in, and Donna was very happy working with children at the school.

As can happen sometimes, when a ministry is going so well, the air of excitement turned to one of uncertainty. One of the deacons called Jerry and Donna one day and told him that the pastor wanted them to rent his house so the pastor and his wife could buy a new home. Jerry and Donna could not afford to rent the house, much less pay the utilities. The house the pastor and his wife were in was a two-story and much-bigger than the house Jerry and Donna lived in. They told the deacon this, and it was relayed to the pastor, and afterward, things began to happen to make Jerry feel insecure about his position.

Soon, Christopher Sean Willis appeared on the scene. He came at a time when there was so much uncertainly for Jerry and Donna. Chris was a very happy baby with a big beautiful smile. He and Mandy were so cute together. Big sister helping take care of her new brother. As Shondra Pierce would put it, "it was so precious." So even though they were facing a giant, the Lord and Mandy and Chris kept them going. Through the years, Chris has learned to play different types of guitars, a violin, and he can sing. He also draws beautiful artwork.

So within a few months, Jerry was asked to leave the church, and they all moved in with us. We lived in a small three-bedroom, one-bath house. There were some hard times but also some good times.

I remember one morning about five o'clock, Donna had dried some clothes. In the process of putting them in the dryer, she dropped one of Chris's socks. All the clothes had dried, except the one sock. Donna came up with what she thought was a perfect idea: she would iron the sock. As Donna was ironing the sock, Joan came down the small hallway and realized what Donna was doing. She asked her, "What are you doing? Don't you know that you don't iron socks?" Well, Donna wanted to know why not, but all Joan could tell her is that her mama didn't do it and she never had. (Yes, we are still a very close and loving family, even during times of sock-tribulation.)

Donna took a job at one of the local churches as membership secretary. At this point, only Joan and Donna were working.

After being at the church for a while, Donna was talking to the headmaster at the school. Come to find out, he and Jerry knew each other. There was an opening at the high school for a history teacher. Long story short, Jerry was interviewed and got the job. That is how Jerry and his family ended back in South Georgia.

After Joan, Jerry, and Donna were all settled with new jobs, the house next to us went up for sale. The price was right, and we ended up purchasing the house. Donna and Jerry lived there for several years.

One day, it was time for everyone to get home. Donna was running a little behind (we had dinner at our house every night). We soon saw her drive up. Everyone else was seated at the dinner table. Donna pulled up and went into their house to change clothes. Jerry, her husband, was such a prankster. You would have loved him. Anyway, as Donna does, she headed to the bathroom and noticed the toilet seat was down. She really didn't think anything about it. She proceeded to get ready, pulled the seat up, dropped the seat, and yelled, "There is a snake in the toilet!" It didn't take Donna long to regroup and realized that the snake in the toilet belonged to Chris. She changed her clothes and marched right on over to our house, flung the door open, and demanded to know who had put the snake in the toilet. By this time, however, everyone was laughing so hard that Donna finally had to chime in. It was Jerry who had put the snake in the toilet.

We are extremely sorry and happy at the same time to say that Jerry went to be with his Lord and Savior Jesus Christ on September 18, 2018. He had been diagnosed with stage 4 prostate cancer about five years prior. The doctor Jerry first saw told him he would only have about a year to live as the cancer had already metastasized to his bones. Jerry preached during these years as much as he could. During the weeks he took Chemotheraphy, he was very sick and weak. He would miss that next Sunday. But the Lord sent Ross and Sandra Powell, our good friends, and Ross preached during these days. They are such a blessing. However, by the grace of God, he lived five years. Jerry was able to preach to his congregation the two Sundays before his passing.

Jerry was first and foremost a Christian, husband, father, teacher, and preacher. He was one of the most compassionate and unselfish people whom you could have ever meet. Donna told us that when they went grocery shopping, the way she would find Jerry when they got separated was to just listen, because Jerry was always happy and he would whistle.

After Billy Graham's death, Jerry wrote this tribute to Dr. Graham:

MY TRIBUTE TO DR. BILLY GRAHAM

As Billy Graham entered the presence of the Lord, he entered not as a famous evangelist, but as a humble servant totally dependent on the salvation of Christ.

He hears "Well Done" not because of his preaching to large crowds, but rather being faithful to his calling.

I will never forget the opportunity to meet you and look into your steel blue eyes which seemed to pierce my soul and you thanking me for my answering "the call" to the Gospel Ministry", when it was me who should be saying, "Thanks Dr. Graham, I look forward to meeting you again and thanking you once more for the impact you had on the life of this farm boy.

Jerry Willis

JERRY, DONNA AND CHRIS WILLIS

Mandy was a very sweet and loving child, and very talented. She started singing when she was very young, and this always thrilled us. Mandy made her first singing appearance when the Dixie Prophets sang at Ed's Truck Stop in Poulan. She did such a wonderful job, and has continued to use her voice for the Lord to this day.

Mandy and Scott Kavanaugh were married in 1997 at the Christ United Methodist Church in Albany. It was such a beautiful, elegant, black-and-white wedding (Scott and Mandy did the decorating). Jerry walked Mandy down the aisle, as well as performed the ceremony. During the ceremony, one of the groomsmen fainted and fell backward and hit the floor. Everyone was afraid he was hurt, but he was able to get up, and the wedding proceeded. He did go to the hospital, and everything was normal.

Scott and Mandy soon had a bubbly, beautiful terrier named Teddy. He was considered Donna and Jerry's grandchild for a while. Jerry and Donna had purchased a new manufactured home. Scott and Mandy called them, and said they needed to come over and tell us something. Being the mother and father, the first thing they thought was that Mandy and Scott were going to tell us they were expecting. Instead, they met Teddy. Teddy became a real part of their family soon. He decided to initiate their new carpet the very day they met him.

Before too long, Mandy found out that she was going to have a baby. Of course, we were all excited. In January 2000, Hannah Grace Kavanaugh made her appearance. She looked so much like Mandy. It was almost as if Mandy was physically being born again.

Then in December 2001, Emily Elizabeth Kavanaugh made an appearance. Her smile did and will light up a room to this day. Both the girls attended private school and were very involved in the arts and sports.

Hannah Grace attends the University of Mobile, in Alabama. She received a music scholarship to that University where she attends today. She had interned at one of largest churches in Nashville, Tennessee, since she graduated from high school, and has worked at a music studio.

And Emily is starting her final year in high school. We know the Lord will direct her down the right path, just as he did for Hannah Grace.

HANNAH GRACE, MANDY, SCOTT AND EMILY KAVANAUGH

Anthony James "Tony" Tucker

We were blessed with another child in 1960. His name is Anthony James "Tony" Tucker. We were living in Moultrie, and he was born at Vereen Memorial Hospital. He was always healthy when he was growing up, with the exception of tonsillitis. When he was about fourteen years of age, he had a tonsillectomy. This surgery was hard on him, but he managed to get through it.

Tony was always a neat person, even in his younger years, who loved to have things real clean. When he first started feeding himself, if he dropped food beside his plate, it had to be cleaned up before he would continue eating.

Since he was the only boy in the family, he always had a bedroom by himself. About once a month he would move all the furniture around and make sure the room was clean. He is pretty much like that to this day.

When Tony was growing up, we went fishing a lot. One day, we were fishing on the Flint River when the wind started to blow. It was blowing extremely hard, and it blew our boat into some trees. We grabbed on to some limbs, trying to hold the boat still. Both of us looked up and saw a big dark moccasin lying on a tree limb. Tony started to get out of the boat. I told him not to do that but to hold on to the tree limb.

Suddenly, the snake fell out of the tree. I really thought he was going to fall into the boat, but he hit the edge of the boat and fell into the water. The wind calmed down, and we moved out into the middle of the river and found a pretty place that was sandy and about waist deep. I threw out the anchor and told Tony, "Let's go swimming." We got out in the water and swam awhile.

After Tony finished high school, he went to work with Larry Langley at his service station in Pelham, Georgia. He was there for quite some time, but finally decided he would go to work with me in the construction business.

While he was working with me, we received a call from Mr. Farmer to do some work at his home. During the time we were there, Mr. Farmer noticed how conscientious Tony was and what a great worker he was. Mr. Farmer called me aside and told me he saw what a good worker Tony was, and he wanted to know if I minded if he talked with Tony about a job with his company. I told him that Tony needed to have a career other than the construction business so that would be fine.

Mr. Farmer asked Tony to meet with him for an interview. After the interview, he hired Tony. This proved to be a very good job. Tony was furnished a new vehicle every year.

This was a great job for him as he had a regular salary, plus all the benefits that he did not have while working in the construction business.

A few years after Tony began employment with Mr. Farmer, he sold his business to a larger marketing company in Birmingham, Alabama.

After going to work with Mr. Farmer, Tony met Bonita Salter Graham. Tony had known the Salters since he was a teenager, but by this time, he was in his late twenties. Tony and Bonita were married in 1989. In 1990, a beautiful blue-eyed baby girl was born into this family. Her name is Jessica Ann Tucker.

When Jessica was around three years old, Tony transferred from Albany to Birmingham, Alabama. They lived in Birmingham for several years. They moved back to Leesburg, Georgia, around 2000.

Tony started a marketing business when he returned to Georgia. He advertised for car dealers in a large area of Georgia, Florida, and Alabama. He was in this business for several years.

The marriage between Tony and Bonita ended in divorce soon after they returned from Birmingham.

Several years after their divorce, Tony met Lori Greene Biery, and they were married in May 2012. Lori has three beautiful girls by her first marriage. They are Alexis Biery Friar, Julia Biery, and Laney Biery.

Lori worked with a company that was closing in 2011. When she was visiting with us, she was talking with Joan about seeking employment. Joan told her to contact our daughter Teri Poitevint, that she had given her resignation and would be leaving Flint Engineering within the next week to accept a job with Pfizer.

Lori called Teri and talked with her about the job. Teri talked with her supervisor, and Lori was asked to come in for an interview. Lori was hired and went to work with Flint Engineering in June 2011. Both Teri and Lori seem to be well suited with both of their jobs.

Lori's oldest daughter, Alexis, married Justin Friar in January 2018 in a beautiful wedding at Chehaw. Justin is youth pastor and Alexis is children's director at Providence

Church in Albany, Georgia. In talking with Lori, she told me that Alexis is clumsy. I told her that I would not put that in the book, but she said that's okay, everybody already knows it.

The next daughter, Julia, is single. She has just begun nurses' training at Albany State College.

She was so excited when she was accepted in this training. She is a person you can depend on for anything.

Tony told me that Julia has the power of healing. He stated she massaged his arm and prayed over it, and it stopped hurting.

Lori's youngest daughter, Laney, is in the tenth grade at Lee County High School, where she is a cheerleader. She is a very sweet and loving girl.

While talking with Tony and Lori, Lori told me that Lily, their granddaughter, is the sweetest girl in the world, and she loves her YaYa and her Papa T.

Tony was approached about employment with Finnicum Motors. He has been employed with them since 2015 and is the finance manager.

Tony and Lori are both very creative. They started buying houses to remodel and flip. They purchased one in 2015 that needed a lot of repair. They remodeled and sold it last year. They have purchased another one and are working on it now. They have completely restored the outside and are now working on the inside.

TONY TUCKER, LANEY BIERY, ALEXIS BIERY
FRIAR, JULIA BERRY AND LORI TUCKER

JUSTIN FRIAR JOINING THE FAMILY

Jessica Ann Tucker and Lily Ann Cross

I talked with our granddaughter Jessica Tucker to get more information about her endeavors. She is such a smart young lady.

Jessica graduated from nursing school in 2014 and began employment in the emergency room at Phoebe Putney Hospital in January 2015. She spent two years at Valdosta State College in Valdosta, Georgia, where she studied biology and took premed courses, finishing all with As and Bs. She has applied to take the Medical College Admissions Test on August 30. She has learned that a new medical school will be opening soon in the Moultrie, Georgia, area. She has asked that we pray, especially on that day, that she will do well on the entrance test.

Jessica states she would like to be an emergency room doctor but is open to whatever will be available to her.

Jessica told me that her daughter, Lily, who will be four in December, is extremely smart. She has been around and is so loved by all the adults in her life and she has learned so much from all of them. She is well adjusted and is a very happy child.

During a visit with Lily and the family, Donna started talking to Lily. Yes, at three, she can carry on a great conversation. Donna gave Lily a dollar while they were talking. Lily showed the dollar around and then came back to Donna. She told Donna she would be giving the dollar to Jesus. What a child!

Tony and Lori had just moved into a new house. Joan and Donna went over to see the house, and our Little Lily was there. Lori asked them if they wanted to see the house. Well, Lori did not show the house, Lily did. She took them into each room and told them whose room it was. It was so cute! I think her calling may be in real estate.

JESSICA ANN TUCKER AND LILY CROSS

Teri Lynn Tucker Poitevint

In 1963, another beautiful baby girl was born into our family. We named her Teri Lynn Tucker.

Teri was born at Vereen Memorial Hospital in Moultrie. Before she was born, Joan had an appointment with Dr. Funderburke one night after eating supper. When he checked Joan's blood sugar, he saw it was elevated. He sent her to the hospital the next morning to have a fasting blood sugar. When we received the results, it was determined the reason for the elevated sugar was she had just eaten a big dinner.

After Teri was born, she had enough fluid in her lungs to fill a water container used in patient's rooms. They drew all the water from her lungs and placed her in an isolette for a few hours. She was ready to go home within a couple of days. We were so afraid she would have some residual from that incident. We were always cautious about making sure everything was done properly.

When she was five years old, she attended kindergarten at Byne Memorial Baptist Church School.

When Teri was six years old, she was enrolled in the first grade at Mock Road Elementary School, since we lived at 2234 Duitman Road in Albany, Georgia. When we moved to another area, she attended Radium Spring Elementary School until she completed the eighth grade. During that time, she was a cheerleader and was popular at school.

Teri and Dean Burke, who was our next-door neighbor, were in the yard playing one day. When she came into the house, she told us that she had hurt her arm. We looked at it, but it didn't look as though anything was wrong except it hurt a little.

A few days later, we looked at Teri's wrist and realized it looked as though the bone was protruding a little. We took her to the doctor. He did x-rays and told us her wrist was broken, and it had already started healing back and it would have to be rebroken in order to set it. We felt so terrible that we had not taken her to the doctor in the beginning, but we really didn't think it was broken. The doctor scheduled surgery for her to have her wrist rebroken and set.

The morning of the surgery, Teri was crying when they were taking her to the operating room, and Joan and I were both a basket case to think about why she was having to have that done. She made it through the surgery okay, and the doctor was successful in setting her wrist, and she has no residuals from the break.

When Teri was a student at Riverview Academy, she asked me if I would escort her to the junior-senior prom. It was a huge honor to escort my daughter to that prom. I asked Teri if she would rather have a boy to escort her, but she said, "No, I want my daddy to take me."

She graduated from high school in 1981. She secured employment at J. C. Penney during her senior year in school, and worked there until after she got married.

In 1982, she met Mike Poitevint at church. It became know that when Teri started dating a boy, she would always ask him if he was a Christian. Some people at church would say if a parent has a son who has not been saved, they should encourage him to date Teri since she would always make sure he has been saved before she would date him.

Teri and Mike married in 1983.

MIKE AND TERI POITEVINT

In 1986, Mike and Teri had a son. His name is Joshua Wayne Poitevint. Josh was so small you could hold him in one hand. He soon started growing, and was a healthy boy.

Josh and I went fishing very often, sometimes at Fort Gaines and other times the Flint River. He was my fishing partner for many years. I loved fishing with him. We would stop by the service station, get crackers and drinks that would last for the rest of the day. We would do our best talking on the water. After fishing, we would clean the fish and put them on ice so they would not ruin.

After Josh finished high school, he went to technical college in Dothan, Alabama, which is only about forty miles from our place at Fort Gaines. He lived at our place during this time, since he loved being near the water, where he would fish during the time he was not studying.

He transferred from Dothan to Americus, Georgia, and completed his training. He is now employed as an airplane mechanic at Warner Robins Air Force Base and lives in Perry.

Josh married Mallory Garmon in April 2016 at Fritz Farm in Cordele, Georgia. It was a perfect day for a wedding.

In April 2018, Rhett Isaiah was born. He is such a happy baby and smiles all the time. He is as cute as he can be.

MALLERY, JOSH AND RHETT

Josh and Mallory with Rhett

Their next child was a beautiful baby girl whose name is Kayla Alyse Poitevint. Kayla was small when she was born. Teri had been very sick with both pregnancies and could eat very little.

Kayla graduated from Georgia Southern University in Statesboro, Georgia.

Kayla married John Miller in January 2016 in a beautiful church in Albany. For several years, Kayla told me that if she ever had a son, she would name him Tucker. And she did just that in December 2016. They had their first son, Tucker Stephen Miller.

John and Kayla had another son in January 2019, named Bennett James Miller. When he was born, the doctors discovered he had galactosemia, which is a genetic disorder that affects how the body breaks down a sugar called galactose. A lot of foods have a small amount of galactose, and it's part of a larger sugar called lactose found in dairy products and in most baby formulas and breast milk. To show how God works, a blood test was performed as required for all new born babies in Georgia. Bloodwork was sent to Atlanta for testing. By the time the results were known, Bennett started acting as if something was wrong. They called Bennett's pediatrician, who had them bring Bennett into the office. Approximately 15 minutes before John and Kayla arrived, the doctor from Atlanta called Bennett's pediatrician regarding the results. Immediately, he was admitted into the hospital until they were able to flush the sugar from his tiny body. He is now on a restricted diet but can live a normal life.

JOHN, TUCKER, BENNETT, AND KAYLA MILLER

Well, this is my family thus far. There could be other little patters of feet later. Only the good Lord knows if that will happen.

My family is everything to me. Of course, God is first, then my lovely wife of 65 years and my three children. Through my children, of course, have come many others. The Lord has given to me a heart big enough to love each and everyone of them. I only have two brothers living and I hope they know how much I love them and think of them often.

I give God the praise and glory for everything and everybody He has put in my path.

I hope you have enjoyed going down memory lane with me. It has been a real exciting time for me and my family to dig back into the past and connect with the future.

Seven Brothers' Military Service

Dolphus Mathew Tucker
US Army

Madison Junior Tucker
US Marine Corps

William James Tucker
US Marine Corps

Wayne Donald Tucker
US Navy

Dewey Ray Tucker
US Air Force

William Larry Tucker
US Navy

Daulton Terry Tucker
US Navy

I would like to dedicate this book to my six brothers who served faithfully in the military. They served their country well, and I am proud of each one.

I would also like to thank my lovely wife and my daughters, Donna and Teri, for all the research to make this book trueful to the best of my knowledge. I want to thank them for the many hours spent gathering information to ensure facts are correct.

I also want my entire family to know that I appreciated the time they spent gathering information for the book.

I Love You All
Bill

About the Author

William J. (Bill) Tucker has been a faithful member of Mercedes Baptist Church since May of 1986. He has served as deacon and sang in the choir. Bill has written numerous songs (some of which are in this book) and poems. The Lord has blessed him with so many talents, including drawing.

If you like a book that makes you laugh, cry, and feel good, read *Coming down the Road with Jesus.*

This is a true story about a boy who grew up on the farm, had seven brothers and three sisters. All the boys served in the military, and a great-granddaddy served as a captain in the militia during the War Between the States, and signed the Georgia Ordinance of Secession in January 1861.

From Great-granddaddy stems many families. From wives, children, and great-grandchildren. There is so much history in each family. So, come along with me and get to know my family. Let's all get together and go down the road with Jesus.

> "There shall not any man be able to stand before thee all the days of thy life: as I was in Moses, so I will be with thee: I will not fail thee, nor forsake thee" (Joshua 1:5 KJV).